READY *to* GIVE *an* ANSWER

A Course in Christian Evidences

DAVID R. REID

Original text material by David R. Reid

Developed as a correspondence course by
Emmaus Correspondence School
founded in 1942

PUBLISHED BY:

ECS Ministries
P.O. Box 1028
Dubuque, IA 52004-1028
www.ecsministries.org

Unless otherwise noted all Bible quotations in this course are from the New King James Version of the Holy Bible © 1982 by Thomas Nelson, Inc., used by permission.

Quotations noted NASB, are taken from the *New American Standard Bible®*, copyright 1960, 1962, 1963, 1968, 1971, 1972, 1973, 1975, 1977, 1995 by The Lockman Foundation, used by permission.

ISBN 0-940293-77-3

123456789/06050403

© 2003 ECS Ministries

Printed in the United States of America

ACKNOWLEDGMENT

My special thanks goes to my wife, Margie, with out whom this course would not have been completed. Margie spent many hours listening to my taped lectures and preparing the text for this course.

Dr. David Reid, a faculty member at Emmaus Bible College for 28 years, is the founder of Growing Christians Ministries. Information about his ministry and his teaching material may be found at www.growingchristians.org.

READY TO GIVE AN ANSWER
INSTRUCTIONS TO STUDENTS

COURSE COMPONENTS

The course has two parts: this textbook and the exam booklet.

The Study Course

The study course contains the material that you will use in your studies.

The Exam Booklet

The exam booklet includes all the exams for the course.

HOW TO STUDY

Begin by asking God to open your heart to receive the truths He would teach you from His Word. Read each chapter of the course book through at least twice, once to get the general idea of its contents and then again, slowly, looking up all Scripture references and examining all footnotes. Remember, you may use a dictionary for any terms you do not understand.

EXAMS

All the exams are in the Exam Booklet. Before taking each exam, carefully review the relevant chapter material including the Bible references. When you actually come to take the exams, try to do so without reference to the chapter, your Bible or your notebook unless otherwise instructed.

STUDY SCHEDULE

Begin studying immediately, or if you are in a group, as soon as the group begins. We suggest that you allow yourself a maximum of one year tom complete this course from the time of enrollment.

READY TO GIVE AN ANSWER
A COURSE IN CHRISTIAN EVIDENCES

TABLE OF CONTENTS

INTRODUCTION

A. WHAT DOES "CHRISTIAN EVIDENCES" MEAN?

What is evidence? We usually think of evidence as things (finger-prints, weapons, stolen articles) or the testimony of people (eyewitnesses) that attorneys present in a court of law in order to convince a judge or jury that their case is true and believable. Christian evidence is just like that, it's evidence which Christians can present in order to convince others that God, the Bible and Christianity are true, and that our faith is reasonable, logical and credible.

When all is said and done, you cannot *prove* Christianity to the point where no faith is needed (see Hebrews 11:6). Becoming a Christian requires faith, no matter how much you know about the evidence for Christianity. But the Christian faith is not a "blind" faith. It's not a "leap out into the dark." It's a logical and reasonable step of faith—a step of faith based on evidence that is solid and credible.

The best kind of evidence that attorneys present in court is objective, physical, verifiable evidence: the written and oral testimony of eyewitnesses, the written testimony of experts on the subject, and exhibits, such as photographs, fingerprints, DNA, videotape, clothing, weapons, etc. In proving the case for Christianity we want to use objective evidence, too. God has given us overwhelming evidence to convince us and others that the Christian faith is logical and grounded in truth. We have exhibits, the written and oral testimony of credible eyewitnesses, and the testimony of expert witnesses to back up our case. If we study the evidences and know how to use them, we will be able to present a good defense every time the case for Christianity is tried! That is what this course is all about.

B. WHY STUDY THE EVIDENCE FOR CHRISTIANITY?

1. To show that Christianity is reasonable, logical and credible.

Christianity is based on historical fact. Historical events are central to Christianity. Some religions or faiths are based entirely on the teachings of their founders (such as Mohammed and Islam, or Joseph Smith and Mormonism). In Christianity, however, both the teachings of Jesus Christ *and* the historical events of His life are essential. In fact, Christianity stands or falls based on the truth of the historical events that are recorded in the Bible, such as the life, miracles, death and resurrection of Jesus Christ.

The Bible stresses the importance of being able to prove these historical events. After His death and resurrection, Jesus appeared to His disciples and "presented Himself alive after His suffering by many infallible proofs, being seen by them during forty days and speaking of the things pertaining to the kingdom of God" (Acts 1:3). Peter says "we . . . were eyewitnesses" (2 Peter 1:16). Paul stated that many people could testify to the accuracy of his message about Jesus, including King Agrippa: "I . . . speak the words of truth and reason. For the king . . . knows these things; for I am convinced that none of these things escapes his attention, since this thing [the death and resurrection of Christ] was not done in a corner" (Acts 26:25-26).

2. To learn how to defend Christianity.

God asks us to defend and confirm the gospel (Philippians 1:7). When the apostle Paul wrote, "I am appointed for the defense of the gospel" (Philippians 1:17), he was a prisoner in Rome, where most of the people were hostile to Christianity. God had placed him in that situation to defend and confirm the gospel in pagan Rome. Jude urged Christians to "contend earnestly for the faith" (Jude 3), and Titus was told to refute the arguments of those who opposed his message (Titus 1:9).

God expects all Christians to be able to defend and confirm the message of the Bible. In fact, He commands us to be ready and able to give answers! "Always be ready to give a defense to everyone who asks you a reason for the hope that is in you" (1 Peter 3:15), and "redeeming the time [make the most of every opportunity] . . . know how you ought to answer each one" (Colossians 4:5-6). We should study evidences of our Christian faith so that we can give answers.

3. To follow the example of the apostles.

The apostles are tremendous examples of how to live and grow in faith, and of how to evangelize and teach others about Christianity. As they used evidences in their teaching and evangelism, so we should be able to use evidences as well.

The apostle Paul stated that creation gives evidence of Godís "invisible attributes . . . eternal power and Godhead [divine nature]" (Romans 1:20). In his speech to King Agrippa, Paul mentioned fulfilled prophecies from the Old Testament as evidence that Jesus is the Messiah (Acts 26:22-27).

In his sermon on the Day of Pentecost, Peter spoke of "Jesus of Nazareth, a man attested by God to you by miracles, wonders, and signs . . . as you yourselves also know" (Acts 2:22). Many of the people to whom he was speaking had personally seen Jesus perform miracles, and at that very moment they were witnessing the amazing signs of the outpouring of the Holy Spirit on the disciples! Peter used the power of these signs and miracles as evidence for the validity of Jesus as the Christ, and 3,000 people believed!

In 1 Corinthians 15:4-6, Paul stated that more than 500 people had seen the Lord Jesus Christ alive after the resurrection. He went on to say that most of those eyewitnesses were still alive, and that they would confirm the truth of the resurrection of Jesus.

Paul wrote to the Philippians, "The things which you learned and received and heard and saw in me, these do [put it into practice!]" (Philippians 4:9). We, too, should follow the pattern set for us by the apostles.

C. WHAT WILL I LEARN IN THIS COURSE?

This brief course will present basic, logical, objective evidences for the existence of God, the deity of Jesus Christ and the reliability of the Bible. It also covers evidence for miracles, Creation, and the world-wide

Flood. In addition, many of the objections which are raised by critics are stated and shown to be incorrect or erroneous. A "Recommended Reading" list is given if you wish to study the subject of evidences in greater depth.

As you study this course, your personal faith will be strengthened, and you will learn to be "ready always to give an answer to every man that asketh you a reason of the hope that is in you" (1 Peter 3:15, KJV).

❖   ❖   ❖

CHAPTER ONE

IS THE BIBLE RELIABLE?

Is the Bible the true, inerrant (without error) and reliable Word of God, or is it a mixture of stories, fables, legends, and half-truths, as some people say? Can we really *trust* the Bible? Is the information it contains about the existence and character of God, the Creation and Fall of mankind, and the means of salvation absolutely correct? Since our faith and our eternal destiny depend on the truthfulness of the Bible, we need to know and be able to present good evidence that the Bible which is in our hands today is authentic and unchanged, and that we can rely on all biblical information to be accurate and trustworthy.

The evidence that we will examine in this chapter falls into four categories: **authenticity**, **accuracy**, **agreement**, and **acceptance** of Scripture. We want to find out whether or not the Bible has changed over the years. Does the Bible contain mistakes? Do the authors contradict or disagree with one another? When were the biblical documents accepted as the true and reliable Word of God? As Christians, we believe that the Bible is completely reliable, of course, because we believe it to be the inspired, inerrant Word of God. But remember, we are presenting this evidence to disprove the skeptic's objections. If the Bible passes the authenticity, accuracy, agreement and acceptance tests, then unbelievers must logically conclude that the Bible is a reliable document, regardless of their views of God and inspiration.

A. AUTHENTICITY: *Has the Bible changed over the years?*

Authenticity is the necessary first step in establishing the reliability of the Bible. When we say a document is "authentic," we mean that the document is **the same as the original** written text— nothing has been **added**, nothing has been **deleted**, and nothing has been **changed**. The original written documents of the Bible (called "autographs") are no longer in existence, and there are no "Xerox copies" available! Have the biblical writings been preserved carefully over the years? How do we find out if the text we have today is a good, accurate, authentic **copy** of the **original** text? To look for evidence, we must find out if the **available ancient copies** of the biblical documents are the **same** as the biblical text we have today. We need to get as close to the original documents as possible.

AUTHENTICITY
ACCURACY
AGREEMENT
ACCEPTANCE

1. Authenticity of the Old Testament text

The Old Testament was written primarily in Hebrew. Extremely careful handwritten copies (manuscripts) of the original writings were made by Jewish scribes. Jewish scribes followed very strict rules to ensure authentic copies of the biblical documents, with nothing added or deleted from the original text. For example, to be sure no mistakes were made, no word could be copied from memory—they copied the text one letter at a time! When a scribe finished a copy he counted the words and the letters to be sure none had been omitted, and made sure that the middle word and the middle letter of the copy were exactly the same as the middle word and letter of the original document. Now that's a good and authentic copy—even before the day of photocopy machines!

The **Dead Sea Scrolls** are the oldest existing copies of the Old Testament documents. In 1947, in a cave near the Dead Sea, a shepherd boy discovered an ancient scroll of the book of Isaiah in a clay jar. Other caves were soon discovered, which contained more scrolls of biblical documents and commentaries (written explanations of the biblical text). The biblical scrolls consisted of handwritten copies of all the books of the Old Testament, except Esther. When compared to the Hebrew text of the Old Testament used today there were only a few minor differences. The oldest of the scrolls may have been made before 200 B.C. All indications are that the Old Testament Hebrew text had not changed between the time the original books were written and the time of the Dead Sea Scrolls.

The **Septuagint** is a translation of the Old Testament from Hebrew into Greek, which was made in about 250 B.C. by Jewish scholars in Alexandria, Egypt. There are many copies of the Septuagint, and when we compare these ancient Greek manuscripts with the Hebrew text, the text is amazingly close to what was found in the Hebrew texts of the Dead Sea Scrolls.

We have other ancient Hebrew manuscripts (the Talmud, Midrash and Targums) that contain Scripture. We also have the Samaritan version of the Pentateuch (the first five books of the Bible), and various archaeological artifacts that contain Hebrew Scripture. All these sources provide good evidence to back up the authenticity of the Hebrew text of the Old Testament. When we check the biblical texts of the Dead Sea Scrolls, Septuagint, and these other ancient sources with the Old Testament we have in our Bibles today, we find that the texts are in substantial agreement. The few differences, which are fairly easy to detect, are very minor scribal copying mistakes, not affecting the doctrine of the Scripture—certainly not **major changes**! We can be confident that the Old Testament in our Bibles today is an **authentic** copy of the original documents.

2. Authenticity of the New Testament text

The New Testament was written in Greek. The oldest manuscript of the **entire** New Testament, found at St. Catherine's Monastery at Mt. Sinai, dates to about 350 A.D. However, there are many **portions** of the New Testament on manuscripts which are dated earlier (and thus closer to the original documents). One of the oldest existing manuscripts of the New Testament is a small portion of the Gospel of John, which was copied in about 125 A.D., only 30-40 years after the original text of the gospel was written by the Apostle John.

There are over 20,000 ancient handwritten manuscripts (more than 5,000 in the Greek language) of the New Testament in existence today, plus more than 86,000 New Testament quotations in early Christian writings. The "Patristic Writings" (commentaries and instructional books written by early Christian leaders, which date back to the 2nd century AD) and "lectionaries" (early church service manuals) quote many passages from the New Testament. In fact, so much Scripture is quoted in these early commentaries and lectionaries that, even if all Bibles were lost, we could reconstruct almost the entire New Testament just from the quotations in these very early Christian writings!

When we compare all these manuscripts, we find some minor differences or variations (called variants), but the vast majority of verses are identical. And in the relatively few variants, no doctrine is involved. In fact, the New Testament manuscripts are considered to be 98.3% in agreement with each other—a literary miracle! Do these documents agree with the New Testament we have today? Yes, they do! We can be confident of the **authenticity** of the New Testament in our Bibles today.

Conclusion: No one doubts the existence of Julius Caesar or the historical information in his book, *Gallic Wars*, even though only 10 manuscripts remain and there is a 900 year gap between the writing of the book and the oldest manuscript copy. The manuscript evidence for the events recorded in the New Testament for the life of Christ is **far** superior to the evidence for the events in the life of Julius Caesar. And manuscript evidence is essentially the only kind of evidence that can be used to establish the historicity of these events. Although skeptics attempt to describe the Bible as a book that has been exaggerated or changed over the years, we have the evidence—the Bible is an **authentic** document!

B. ACCURACY: *Are there mistakes in the Bible?*

Having established that the Bible we have today is an **authentic copy of the original documents**, and has not been changed since the time it was written, we need to go further and look at evidence to show that what the authors originally wrote was **correct** and **accurate**. The Bible claims to be the Word of God and therefore, as Christians, we accept its accuracy. But in this course we want to learn how to show the skeptic that the Bible does not contain errors. Luke, for example, has been demonstrated to be an accurate historian. Luke stated that his specific purpose in writing his books was "to write to you an orderly account . . . that you may know the certainty of those things in which you were instructed" (Luke 1:3-4). We will look at several areas of biblical accuracy.

AUTHENTICITY
ACCURACY
AGREEMENT
ACCEPTANCE

1. Scientific Accuracy

Some critics of the Bible claim that the Bible has many scientific inaccuracies. Much of the criticism arises from the fact that the Bible is written in the language and from the viewpoint of common, ordinary people, using popular expressions. For example, a critic might say that the phrase "the sun rises and the sun sets" in Ecclesiastes 1:5 (NASB) is a scientific error, because the **sun** doesn't move around the earth—the **earth** rotates! They also allege that the phrase "the four corners of the earth" in Isaiah 11:12 is a scientific mistake made by an author who thought the world was flat. But it's quite obvious that "the sun rises and sets" is simply the common phrase used then (and today!) to describe the day from dawn to dusk, and the "four corners of the earth" is just a descriptive phrase for "the whole world." After all, the purpose of the Bible is not to teach science, and the language of the Bible is not **meant** to be scientific!

When the meaning of words and phrases in the original language are examined more carefully, other alleged "scientific mistakes" are often found not to be mistakes at all. In fact, there are certain Scriptures in which the inspired writers may go "beyond the knowledge of their time" and use language that is **more** scientifically accurate than they ever realized! For example, that fact that the earth is a sphere may be included in Isaiah 40:22, which was written hundreds of years before the earth was proved to be a sphere. The great wind circuits that circle the earth and the earth's hydraulic cycle that are mentioned in Ecclesiastes 1:6-7 were probably beyond the scientific knowledge of Solomon's day.

Although the purpose of the Bible is not to teach science, where the Bible touches on science there are **no mistakes**! God's Word **is** scientifically accurate!

2. Medical Accuracy

The medical advice and information given in ancient literature is filled with gruesome myths and ridiculous therapies, but the Bible is different. Where the Bible mentions medical matters, it does not make mistakes. Many of the rules of God's Law in the Old Testament were given to protect the health of His people, even though the people then didn't know the medical principles behind the regulations.

When we compare those rules with the medical knowledge of today, we see that the "clean and unclean" laws were very important for preventing contagious diseases and promoting good health. One amazing example is found in Leviticus 12:3, which required Jewish baby boys to be circumcised on the 8th day after birth. We now know that Vitamin K, a substance which is necessary for blood to clot, naturally reaches its peak in an infant's body when the baby is 8 days old! There are similar examples throughout the Bible. Paul's advice to Timothy to ". . . use a little wine for your stomach's sake and your frequent infirmities" (1 Timothy 5:23) is not an outdated "old wives' tale." Medical research has found that drinking a little wine with meals is helpful in combating intestinal illnesses carried by food and water—and it may help to prevent heart attacks as well! (Incidentally, 1 Timothy 5:23 is not making a statement on social drinking—it is medical advice.) These are just a couple of examples of biblical health regulations or therapies that have been "re-discovered" and validated by current medical research and knowledge. God's Word is medically accurate!

3. Historical, Geographical and Prophetic Accuracy

A study of Bible geography, history and prophecy will show that the Bible is accurate down to the smallest details. This evidence will be discussed in more detail in Chapters 2 and 3.

C. AGREEMENT: *Do the human authors of the Bible agree?*

The Bible is composed of 66 books, written over a period of about 1,500 years by more than 40 authors of different ages, from different backgrounds and walks of life, using different literary forms, and yet there is amazing harmony among the authors of Scripture! While critics attempt to point out small details that **seem** to disagree, generally these are only **apparent** or surface "contradictions." With careful examination, the criticisms of **all** these alleged contradictions can be resolved.

AUTHENTICITY
ACCURACY
AGREEMENT
ACCEPTANCE

A few very brief examples are as follows:

1. **Criticism:** Genesis 1:26-27 and Genesis 2:7, 21-22 are contradictory accounts of the creation of man and woman.

Answer: Genesis 1 is a summary statement of the creation of humans, and Genesis 2 gives a more detailed account—**how** God did it.

2. **Criticism:** The genealogies (family records) of the Old Testament are not always in agreement.

Answer: Sometimes biblical chronologies are shortened or condensed. This was not unusual in ancient times, and does not make the genealogy untrue.

3. Criticism: John's account of Jesus "cleansing the Temple" comes at the **beginning** of Jesus' public ministry, while Matthew, Mark and Luke give a "Temple cleansing" account at the **end** of Jesus' ministry.

Answer: Jesus cleansed the Temple on two different occasions. Read the accounts, and you will see some significant differences in the descriptions of the two cleansings.

4. Criticism: The number of men and the location are different in the account of the healing of the blind man/men near Jericho in the three gospels that record it. In Luke 18:35, **one** blind man was healed as Jesus was **entering** Jericho. In Mark 10:46 a blind man named Bartimaeus was healed as Jesus **left** Jericho. In Matthew 20:30, **two** blind men were healed as Jesus **left** Jericho.

Answer: No problem!
a. **The number of men**—there were two blind men who were healed, but Mark and Luke chose to mention only one of them, probably the one who did the talking. Mark even gives his name: Bartimaeus.
b. **The location**—One possible solution is that the healings took place between the two locations of Jericho. There was more than one Jericho—an Old Testament location, which was conquered by Joshua, and a New Testament location, where Herod had a palace. Matthew and Mark, who were Jewish writers and raised in the Hebrew tradition, wrote that the healings took place as Jesus was leaving the locale of the Old Testament Jericho. Luke, the Gentile writer, wrote that the man was healed as Jesus was approaching New Testament Jericho. One other possibility: The request for healing came as He was entering New Testament Jericho, and the actual healing took place as He left New Testament Jericho.

5. Criticism: The accounts of the resurrection of Jesus differ in the different Gospels.

Answer: Each writer gives his own account of the events from his own perspective, so that each includes different details of information. All the information can be harmonized, and a complete account of the resurrection presented. The fact that there **are** differences in their accounts is actually a strong indication that the authors did not collaborate, or get together to concoct a fictitious resurrection story!

D. ACCEPTANCE: *When, and by whom, was the text accepted as true?*

If it can be shown that a document was accepted as a true and reliable account from the time of the recorded events, this is a powerful argument for the reliability of the record. For example, just try to get people today to believe a reconstructed history of World War II—including the United States General Dwight Eisenhower miraculously healing the injured, or the British Prime Minister Winston Churchill parting the waters of the English Channel to bring troops across to France—and see if your document is accepted by many! This is one of the best ways to demonstrate that the criticism of the Bible by the skeptics is far-fetched.

AUTHENTICITY
ACCURACY
AGREEMENT
ACCEPTANCE

1. Old Testament

The Old Testament text, miracles and all, was accepted as the true and reliable and authoritative Word of God as far back as we can trace the documents or the people.

a. By the Jewish people

i. The Jewish people accepted the Old Testament documents in their entirety from the time they were written.
ii. If the written information had been completely false, the Jewish people would have rejected the documents immediately—but they did not reject them.
iii. If the documents had been only partially true, with some historical or numerical errors, for example, the Jewish people would have revised and corrected them—but there is absolutely no shred of evidence that this ever happened. If the documents were not entirely reliable, the Jewish people would have simply denied that they were truly Scripture. For example, the Jewish people never accepted the intertestamental books called the "Apocrypha" as Scripture.

iv. Even when the Jewish people didn't like the contents of a book (such as the many messages of judgment on the Jewish people themselves), they still accepted the documents as the true Word of God.

b. By Jesus Christ

i. Jesus accepted and quoted the Old Testament as reliable and true. For example, Jesus referred to the Genesis accounts of Creation (Matthew 19:4-6), the worldwide Flood (Matthew 24:37-39), and the story of Jonah (Matthew 12:40-41). He obviously considered these accounts to be true, even though many people today dismiss them as mere fables or Jewish mythology.
ii. If Jesus accepted the Old Testament as true, and it is not true, then either Jesus was ignorant and didn't know the stories were only legends, or else He knowingly "went along" with the legends and was thus a deliberate deceiver.

2. New Testament

The New Testament text, including the miracles and the resurrection of Jesus Christ, was accepted as the true Word of God by the early Christians.

a. In a short time

i. Even while the New Testament was still being written, Christians believed that the information in the documents was true and reliable, and accepted the documents as **Scripture**. (See 2 Peter 3:15-16). Other books written around this time, called New Testament apocryphal and pseudepigraphal writings, were not accepted as true and reliable by the early Christians.
ii. The time gap between the events and the time when the records were written is short—it is certainly too short for gross exaggerations or obvious errors to have been inserted. (See Acts 26:25-26.)
iii. Eyewitnesses to the events recorded in the Gospels and Acts were still alive when the documents were written (see 1 Corinthians 15:6), and these witnesses would have certainly denied any exaggerated or falsified account. Furthermore, they would have corrected any of the documents that were only partially true. But there is no evidence that any documents were ever revised.

b. In spite of persecution

Some of the early Christians were imprisoned and even executed for their faith. Is it possible that so many people would be willing to suffer persecution, torture and death for a lie, when they **knew** it was a lie? (See Acts 4:1-3; 5:17-18; 7:57-60; 12:1-4 for a few examples.)

CONCLUSION

The Bible is unique. It is a book with the stamp of its supernatural Authorship clearly upon it. Despite the fact that it consists of 66 books, written by a wide variety of human authors over a period of at least 1,500 years, the Bible is a unified book. The writers tell **one** story: the message of God, who loves people enough to personally provide a plan of salvation for them.

AUTHENTICITY
ACCURACY
AGREEMENT
ACCEPTANCE

Compared to other ancient documents, the Bible is **incredibly** reliable. And if it is accurate in every area that we **can** check, we can be confident that the Bible tells the truth about areas we **can't** check. It speaks with authority on otherwise unknowable subjects, such as heaven, hell, angels, demons, the character of God, and eternity past and future, thus displaying its supernatural origin.

The fact that the Bible is still in existence today is further evidence that it is a supernatural book. Over the centuries it's been hated, banished, suppressed, and burned, but the Bible is still here and by far the "best seller" book the world has ever known. And its message is still changing lives!

❖   ❖   ❖

CHAPTER TWO

DOES ARCHEOLOGY SUPPORT THE BIBLE?

Archaeology (the study of ancient peoples and their cultures) has produced a tremendous amount of evidence that supports the historical and geographical accuracy and reliability of the Bible. In fact, archaeology has uncovered *nothing* which contradicts the Bible! Archaeological findings have closed the mouths of critics who had declared that many of the Bible's historical facts were merely legends. In this chapter we have space to mention only a few of the many findings which support the Old and New Testament texts.

A. WHAT IS ARCHAEOLOGY?

1. **Definition:** The science of archaeology studies past human life and activities by examining "artifacts" (material products made by humans) of ancient cultures. The remains of ancient cities, dwellings, tools, agricultural and household implements, weapons, religious artifacts, coins, etc., are studied to gain information about the existence and culture of ancient civilizations.

2. **Digging:** Although some archaeological studies are done above ground (the Pyramids, for example), most archaeological work involves digging underground to expose the remains of past civilizations or cultures. Archaeological "digs" in Israel and other parts of the Middle East are constantly uncovering material from Biblical times.

3. Dating: Determining the correct time period for ancient towns and artifacts is a very important part of archaeology. Particular characteristics of architecture or styles of artifacts are distinctive for each time period in a civilization, and provide clues that are used for dating. Dating methods include detecting differences in design and decoration (of pottery, lamps, jewelry, etc.), identifying types of metals (in tools or weapons), recognizing architectural trends (of homes, temples, city walls and gates), decoding or translating engravings (inscriptions or coins), etc. Radioactive carbon testing can be used to date anything which was previously living, such as wood, grain, bone, cloth, etc. Since the Bible contains many dates, correct archaeological dating is especially important if we want to use evidence from archaeology to support the accuracy of the Bible.

B. ARCHAEOLOGICAL EVIDENCE OF OLD TESTAMENT ACCURACY

1. Writings or Inscriptions

a. **The Ebla Tablets** (written as early as 2300 B.C., not too long after the Tower of Babel!) mention Sodom and Gomorrah, which were thriving cities at that time. The discovery of these very ancient tablets silenced many biblical critics, who said that the Genesis records couldn't possibly be true because people could not read or write at that "stage of human history"!

b. **The Mari Tablets** (inscribed about the 18th century B.C.) mention customs of that time which are also mentioned in the Bible, including the solemn covenant ritual recorded in Genesis 15.

c. **The Nuzi Tablets** (inscribed about 1500 B.C.) mention several customs described in the Bible, which critics of the Bible formerly questioned. These tablets describe making a servant the heir (Genesis 15), the begetting of an heir through a slave woman (Genesis 16), the sale of a birthright (Genesis 25), and the fact that "household idols" were not just religious objects—in those days they were also title deeds to property. This explains Laban's anxiety to get his missing "household idols" back (Genesis 31).

d. **The Ras Shamra Tablets** (written about 1500 B.C.) describe the grossly immoral religious practices of the Canaanite peoples. To preserve His people from involvement in this type of sin when they entered the Promised Land, God told the Israelites to completely destroy the Canaanites (Deuteronomy 7:1-6). The Ras Shamra tablets support the biblical record of Canaanite wickedness.

e. **Temple of Amon at Karnak**. Inscriptions on the walls of this Egyptian temple (from about 1450 B.C.) list many of the cities mentioned in Numbers 33.

f. **The Amarna Letters** (written about 1400 B.C.) are letters from a Canaanite ruler, asking Egypt for help in fighting an invasion from the "Habiru" people. From 1 Kings 6:1 we know that Joshua and the people of Israel entered the "Promised Land" in about 1400 B.C. "Habiru" is descriptive of nomadic peoples (remember the Israelites were wanderers at this time), and may be related to the name "Hebrew."

g. **The Moabite Stone** (inscribed about 850 B.C.) tells of the conflict between Israel and Moab after the death of Ahab, recorded in 2 Kings 1:1 and 3:5. French professor Andre Lemaire, who has worked on restoring the inscription, states that "This inscription easily establishes the importance of Israel and Judah on the international scene at this time."

h. **The Lachish Reliefs and Sennacherib's Prism** (about 700 B.C.) are Assyrian records which corroborate and support the accounts of the Assyrian invasion of Judah recorded in 2 Kings 18-19, 2 Chronicles 32 and Isaiah 36-37.

i. **Seal of Gemariah** Clay seals (or bullae) originally sealed important documents. A seal found in Jerusalem in 1980 bears the name of Gemariah, son of Shaphan. King Jehoiakim destroyed the scroll of Jeremiah against the advice of his scribe, Gemariah (Jeremiah 36). The name of Jeremiah's scribe, Baruch, also has been found on a 6th century bulla.

j. **The Babylonian Chronicles** (7th-6th century B.C.) tell of the fall of Nineveh in 612 BC, as predicted in the book of Nahum. They also describe the Babylonian assault on Jerusalem in 597 B.C., in which the prophet Ezekiel was captured and taken to Babylon.

k. **The Elephantine Papyrus** (late 5th century B.C.), a document found on Elephantine Island in Egypt, states that Sanballat was governor of Samaria under the Persian Empire, exactly as recorded in Nehemiah 2-6.

2. Archaeological sites

a. **Ur**: Ur, the city where Abraham was born and called by God, has been uncovered and is shown to have been a large, advanced city at Abraham's time (Genesis 11). It was a very idolatrous city, extravagant in its worship of false gods. Ziggurats (towers from which worship of the heavens was conducted) have been found in Ur, Babylon and other places in Iraq. The Tower of Babel was likely an early ziggurat.

b. **Haran:** Genesis 12:4-5 mention that Abraham traveled through Haran on his way to Canaan. Archaeologists have found that Haran was a thriving city at the time of Abraham.

c. **Laish** (later re-named **Dan**): Laish, a Canaanite city in northern Israel, is mentioned in Genesis 14:14. A mud brick city gate has been discovered there, which is dated to Canaanite times. It was preserved because it was purposely buried, and thus it was not destroyed. Archaeological finds indicate that the city plan was probably changed at the time of the Judges, supporting the biblical record of the tribe of Dan's conquest of Laish (Judges 18:27-28).

d. **Jericho:** Old Testament Jericho has been excavated several times. The so-called "problem" of the fallen walls has finally been resolved, in support of the biblical account. Radioactive dating of grain and burned material support the biblical date of the conquest of Canaan by the Israelites about 1400 B.C. (1 Kings 6:1 gives the date of the Exodus as about 1447 B.C. since Solomon began his reign around 971B.C.)

e. **"City of David":** Remains of early Jerusalem from Canaanite times and Israelite times have been found. Both the water shaft mentioned in 2 Samuel 5:8 (about 1000 B.C.), and Hezekiah's tunnel referenced in 2 Kings 20:20 (about 700 B.C.) have been found. The tunnel, an incredible feat of engineering, supplied water from the Gihon Spring (outside the city walls) to the Pool of Siloam (inside the walls). The pick marks of Hezekiah's workmen can still be seen in the bedrock walls of the tunnel. Structures and artifacts have been found in the city of David from the times both before and after the Babylonian exile (6th century B.C.), including a portion of Nehemiah's rebuilt city wall.

f. **Hazor:** Hazor, a major city in northern Israel was conquered and destroyed by fire during the conquest of Canaan (Joshua 11:10-11). It was rebuilt and was again destroyed by Deborah and Barak (Judges 4). Excavations by Israeli archaeologist Yigael Yadin found evidence which confirms the dates and details of both biblical accounts. Recent excavations have uncovered a Canaanite palace, which was probably the palace of Jabin (Judges 4).

g. **Hazor, Megiddo and Gezer:** 1 Kings 9:15 states that these cities were fortified by Solomon. Using this Scripture, Israeli archaeologist Yigael Yadin correctly predicted the type of walls and gates he would find at Megiddo. The Bible proved to be completely accurate!

    h. Dan: The "high place," where pagan worship took place, and where King Jeroboam I set up one of the golden calf shrines (1 Kings 12), has been found at tel Dan. An inscription mentioning a king of "the House of David" was discovered at Dan in 1993. The information on this inscription probably refers to the event in 1 Kings 15:20. This was one of the first discoveries of a mention of David outside the Bible, and it confirms his historical existence.

    i. Nineveh: The site of Nineveh, the capital of the ancient Assyrian Empire, was finally found in the 20th century, confirming the Bible's accurate accounts of this city after years of criticism.

    j. Babylon: Ancient Babylon, the capital of the Babylonian Empire, has been excavated. In fact, the location of the famous Hanging Gardens of Babylon (one of the Seven Wonders of the Ancient World) has been found. Daniel 4:30 records that King Nebuchadnezzar boasted, "Is not this great Babylon, that I have built for a royal dwelling by my mighty power. . . ."

C. ARCHAEOLOGICAL EVIDENCE OF NEW TESTAMENT ACCURACY

    1. Synagogues at Nazareth and Capernaum: The floors of the ancient synagogues that date to the time of Jesus have been uncovered (underneath the ruins of the 4th century synagogues) at Nazareth and Capernaum. Here Jesus read Scripture, taught and healed (Mark 1, Luke 4). During excavations at Capernaum, the remains of an early Christian (Byzantine) church were uncovered, under which a 1st century house was found. Because of Christian symbols found on the walls of the house, and the fact that an early church was built over it to enshrine it, it is thought that this house may have been the actual home of the disciple Peter where the early Christians met together.

    2. The Pool of Bethesda: This pool, mentioned in John 5, has been excavated near the Temple area. Pagan cultic artifacts were also found, which may explain the belief that sick persons would be healed when the "waters were stirred."

    3. The Temple at the time of Christ ("Herod's Temple" or the "Second Temple"): The Jewish Temple was one of the wonders of the ancient world. In Mark 13, Jesus predicted that this magnificent structure would be destroyed, and that not one stone would be left upon another.

The Temple was torn apart in 70 A.D. when the Roman armies put down a major Jewish rebellion. Not one stone of the Temple was left upon another. Much of the platform on which the Temple and its courtyards were built was destroyed. Many huge building stones have been uncovered in archaeological excavations. The bottom layers of this platform are still standing today, and the western wall of the Temple platform (sometimes called the "Wailing Wall") is the principal place of prayer for Jews in Jerusalem today.

4. **Capernaum, Bethsaida** and **Chorazin**: Because of their unbelief, Jesus pronounced judgment on these bustling lakeside towns (Matthew 11). All three towns were destroyed by earthquakes and have never been inhabited since. They have been excavated by archaeologists and the ruins can be seen today.

5. **Caiaphas**: Critics have claimed that Caiaphas, the High Priest at the time of Jesus (John 18:13-14), never existed. However, a 1st century burial cave and an ossuary (a small coffin for bones) inscribed with the name "Caiaphas" were discovered in Jerusalem in 1990. The remains of a large building, with dungeons beneath, have been uncovered near the southern end of the Temple Mount. This site has been identified as possibly the house of Caiaphas (Luke 22:54), where the Lord was held in custody before His trial.

6. **Pontius Pilate**: During the excavation of a Roman theater at Caesarea in 1961, a stone slab with an inscription including the Latin name "Pontius Pilatus" was found. This inscription and the writings of the Jewish historian, Josephus Flavius, corroborate the Bible's record of the Roman governor, Pontius Pilate.

7. **The Gabbatha** ("Pavement"): A Roman pavement of large stone paving blocks has been found in the area where the Antonia Fortress was located in Jerusalem. Grooves are cut in some of the stones to help prevent Roman chariots from skidding on wet pavement. Engravings on the paving stones have been identified as a Roman gambling game called "the game of the king" (see John 19:23). In John 19:13 we read that Jesus was tried at "The Pavement" Although the pavement we see today is dated to the time of the Roman emperor Hadrian (about 100 years after Christ), this may well have been the location.

8. **Baptismal pools**: A "mikvah" was a small pool for Jewish ceremonial washings. Many of these pools have been excavated near the southern steps to the Temple Mount. Quite possibly the 3,000 new converts on the Day of Pentecost were baptized in these pools (Acts 2:41).

9. The **Theater** and the **Temple of Artemis:** These buildings, mentioned in Acts 19, have been excavated in the ruins of the ancient city of Ephesus.

10. **Paul's voyage to Rome:** The historical information given by Luke in his description of Paul's sea voyage to Rome (Acts 27-28) was investigated by experts in historical geography, and was found to be extremely accurate, down to the smallest details of geography and the navigation of that day.

CONCLUSION

Archaeological evidence has confirmed and supported the Bible. The historical information in the Bible is **so** accurate that it has actually assisted archaeologists in their work. Nelson Glueck, a renowned Jewish archaeologist, has stated that no archaeological discovery has ever disproved a biblical reference! The evidence from archaeology assures us that we can **rely** on the **accuracy** of the historical and geographical information in the Bible.

❖   ❖   ❖

ARE BIBLE PROPHECIES ACCURATE?

Fulfilled prophecy is very powerful evidence for the reliability of the Bible. Prophecy is the prediction of events in the future. Fulfilled biblical prophecies are events foretold in the Bible, which we know and can prove have already taken place in history. There are a great many long-range predictions in the Bible, especially in the Old Testament. If we can show that these prophecies in the ancient biblical manuscripts were written before the predicted events took place, and that the prophecies came true just as predicted, we can demonstrate the accuracy of the Bible. The supernatural character of the Bible is also demonstrated, because foretelling details of the future with perfect accuracy is not a natural human ability!

In their efforts to deny that the Bible is a supernatural book, critics of the Bible have disputed the date at which the prophecies were written, claiming that other authors inserted the prophecies into the biblical text **after** the events took place. The discovery of the **Dead Sea Scrolls** in 1947 was crucial in confirming the early date of the Old Testament prophecies. As we saw in Chapter 1, these scrolls are copies of the Old Testament Scriptures, and date to at least 150 B.C. All the evidence points to the fact that the original documents were written much earlier, and there is no indication in the Dead Sea Scrolls that the texts of the Old Testament (including the prophecies) were tampered with or revised in any way after the time they were originally written. The scrolls were copied following rigid rules to ensure accuracy; then, for safekeeping, they were reverently and carefully hidden in remote desert caves. They lay hidden, untouched and unaltered, for almost two thousand years.

All the prophetic books of the Old Testament are included in the Dead Sea Scrolls. Even the most radical and extreme critics of the Bible have to admit that the Dead Sea Scrolls were in existence by 150 B.C., and insertions could not have been added after that time! Since many of the Old Testament prophecies were fulfilled after 150 B.C. (including the many prophecies about the coming of the Messiah), the predictions are, unquestionably, the valid foretelling of future events.

Included in this chapter are just a few of the Old Testament predictions which have already occurred. Clearly, fulfilled prophecies are very reliable evidence that the Bible is accurate.

A. THE MIRACLE OF ISRAEL

Here is a small selection of partly or completely fulfilled prophecies about the miraculous nation of Israel:

1. The miracle of a great nation, through whom blessing would come to all the earth:

Genesis 12:2-3— "I will make you a great nation; I will bless you and make your name great . . . and in you all the families of the earth shall be blessed."

This prophecy was made to Abraham in about 2000 B.C., before Abraham had children. The prophecy was written down by Moses sometime prior to 1400 B.C., before the nation of Israel even existed, and Abraham's descendants were only a "rag-tag" group of people traveling through the wilderness! A skeptic might claim that this prophecy was inserted later (and remember, it would have had to be inserted before 150 B.C., because it's in the Dead Sea Scrolls). If so, when was this inserted? Was Israel ever a nation that brought "blessing to all the earth" prior to the time of the Dead Sea Scrolls? No! But even the critic must agree that blessing has come to this world as a result of the Jewish Messiah, Jesus Christ, and Judeo-Christian values. This is indeed an amazing prediction.

2. The miracle of many descendants who would positively affect all nations:

Genesis 22:17-18— "I will multiply your descendants as the stars of the heaven and as the sand which is on the seashore . . . In your seed all the nations of the earth shall be blessed . . ."

Although the Jewish people are widespread and numerous today, when this prophecy was spoken by God to Abraham in about 2000 B.C., Abraham certainly didn't have numerous descendants—he had only 2 children! Again, when this event was written down by Moses, Abraham's descendants were nomads in the wilderness. They were not "as numerous as the stars," and they certainly were not yet a blessing to all the nations on earth! In fact, this prediction wasn't yet fulfilled when Genesis was copied by the scribes who produced the Dead Sea Scrolls. But even the skeptic must admit that this prophecy has come true. The Jewish people have never ceased to exist. In spite of constant persecution their numbers are innumerable, and great blessing has flowed to the nations of the earth because of Jesus. For example, just think of how the teachings of Jesus, the Jewish Messiah, have resulted in health care and education ministries of Christian missions around the world.

3. The miracle of Jewish preservation in spite of persecution and dispersion (scattering):

Deuteronomy 28:64-66— "Then the LORD will scatter you among all peoples, from one end of the earth to the other . . . And among those nations you shall find no rest . . . Your life shall hang in doubt before you; you shall fear day and night, and have no assurance of life."

Persecution of the Jews has been constant throughout history, but this prophecy was made in 1400 B.C., when the Jews had not even gained a national identity and land. The skeptic is forced to admit that the Nazi Holocaust is just **one** example of the fulfillment of this prophecy since 150 B.C. (the time of the Dead Sea Scrolls).

4. The miracle of preservation of Jewish identity, over hundreds of years, with no national or religious center:

Hosea 3:4— "For the children of Israel shall abide many days without king or prince, without sacrifice or sacred pillar, without ephod or teraphim [idols]."

Since the days of the Jews' captivity in Babylon in the 5th century B.C., there has been no king in Israel. And since the destruction of Jerusalem by the Romans in 70 A.D. there has been no Temple or sacrificial system or priesthood in Israel, yet Jewish culture and customs remain distinct.

5. The miracle of preservation of Jewish identity in spite of dispersion around the world:

Jeremiah 30:10-11— The Lord declared, "I will save you from afar, and your seed from the land of their captivity . . . I am with you . . . to save you. Though I make a full end of all nations where I have scattered you, yet I will not make a complete end of you."

This prophecy was written in about 600 B.C. Other ancient nations have vanished completely, but the Jewish people have never lost their identity, in spite of all the efforts that have been made to destroy them. Critics who try to claim that this prophecy was written during the period of time between the Old and New Testaments (about 400 years) must ignore or deny the evidence of its early origin from the Dead Sea Scrolls! Even if we allow the extreme skeptics to take the position that this prophecy was not written until the time of the Dead Sea Scrolls, these critics cannot deny the amazing accuracy of this prophecy since that time.

6. The miracle of Jews returning to the land of Israel from all nations:

Deuteronomy 30:3-5— "the LORD your God will bring you back from captivity . . . and gather you again from all the nations where the Lord your God has scattered you . . . Then the LORD your God will bring you to the land which your fathers possessed, and you shall possess it. He will prosper you and multiply you more than your fathers."

This prophecy was given through Moses in about 1400 B.C., when the nation of Israel didn't possess even one tiny piece of land! How could anyone dare to write such a prophecy, even as late as the time of the Dead Sea Scrolls? However, the critic of the Bible must agree that the ancient prophecy has been and is being fulfilled.

The return of Israel to its historic land is unique in history. After nearly 2000 years of nonexistence as a nation, its people scattered and intermingled with many nations, and persecuted throughout the dispersion, Jews have returned during this past century and established a nation, revived their ancient language and even their ancient currency!

Isaiah 11:11-12— "the LORD shall set His hand again the second time to recover the remnant of His people who are left . . . and gather together the dispersed of Judah from the four corners of the earth."

This prophecy is one of the most amazing predictions in the Bible, predicting that the Jews would be dispersed from their land and return, not once, but **twice**. This prophecy was written in about 700 B.C. The Jews were indeed driven from their land in 586 B.C. by the Babylonian armies, but this prophecy is not describing the return of the Jews from captivity in 538 B.C. At that **first** return they returned **only from Babylon**, not from the "four corners of the earth." The Jews were again driven from their homeland by the armies of Rome in 70 A.D. Isaiah 11:11-12 predicts a **second** return of the Jews to the land of Israel, this time from **all over the earth**, a return which is taking place in our time!

7. The miracle of Jews resettling Israel and the land regaining its prosperity:

Ezekiel 36:33-35— The Lord says, "I will also enable you to dwell in the cities, and the ruins shall be rebuilt. The desolate land shall be tilled . . . So they will say, 'This land that was desolate has become like the garden of Eden; and the wasted, desolate, and ruined cities are now . . . inhabited.'"

This prophecy, written in about 580 B.C., is partially fulfilled in the land of Israel today, and will continue to be fulfilled until the Lord returns. Ancient towns have been resettled. Land which was desperately poor desert or swamp land ("wasted and desolate") prior to the early 1900's has been irrigated and cultivated, and is now fertile and incredibly productive. Skeptics of the Bible must admit that if this is not an inspired prophecy, then the writer was amazingly "lucky" to have guessed such a stunning "coincidental fulfillment"! The skeptics must acknowledge that Ezekiel was written before the time of the Dead Sea Scrolls—that is, at least before 150 B.C.!

B. THE HISTORY OF CITIES

Some of the Old Testament prophecies about nations and cities have been dramatically fulfilled, while others have not been completely fulfilled yet. Here are a few examples of predictions about ancient cities that have already been fulfilled.

1. **Tyre:** Tyre was a city on the Mediterranean coast in the nation of Phoenicia (where Lebanon is today). In 590 B.C. Ezekiel predicted the destruction of Tyre in great and accurate detail. Look up Ezekiel 26.

a. The mainland city of Tyre was destroyed by Nebuchadnezzar in 573 B.C. "I will bring against Tyre . . . Nebuchadnezzar king of Babylon . . . he will break down your towers . . . he will trample all your streets . . ." (verses 7-11).

b. The well-fortified island city of Tyre was defeated by Alexander the Great in 330 B.C., who scraped the rubble from the mainland city into the Mediterranean Sea to make a causeway to the island: ". . . they will lay your stones, your timber, and your soil in the midst of the water" (verses 12-13).

c. After the smaller, rebuilt city was conquered by Muslim armies in 1291 A.D., Tyre was destroyed. The modern city of Tyre is not on the same location as the ancient city, which has never been rebuilt since its final destruction: ". . . you shall never be rebuilt" (verse 14).

d. The ancient site of Tyre is now a fishing area: ". . . you shall be a place for spreading nets" (verse 14).

2. **Sidon:** Sidon was another town in Phoenicia (Lebanon). Read Ezekiel 28:22-23 and notice the prediction that blood will flow in the streets and "the sword" will be "against her on every side." Over the years there has been a lot of bloodshed in Sidon. From Persian times, when 40,000 Sidonians committed suicide rather than surrender to the Persian army, to the Greek invasion in 330 B.C., through the Muslim/Crusader period when Sidon was conquered and re-conquered six times, right down to present-day conflicts in Lebanon, there has been "blood in the streets" of Sidon.

3. **Petra:** This well-fortified ancient city, carved out of towering red sandstone cliffs, was the wealthy and populous capital of Edom and a major center for trade. Petra flourished even into the Roman period, but is now a "ghost town" and an archaeological site in the present-day nation of Jordan. Read Isaiah 34:5-11 and Jeremiah 49:17-18. As predicted, Petra is deserted except for tourists and wild animals. Ezekiel 35 said that trade and travel would cease in Petra, and Obadiah predicted that Petra

would be "brought down." All of these predictions are contained in the copies of the scrolls of Isaiah, Jeremiah, Ezekiel and Obadiah, which were found in Dead Sea Scrolls, but they were not fulfilled until **long after** the date of the Scrolls. Petra is an excellent example of evidence for the prophetic accuracy of the Bible.

4. **Samaria**: Samaria was the capital of the northern kingdom of Israel. In about 700 B.C., Micah 1:6-7 predicted that Samaria would become a "heap of rubble" and vineyards would grow in the ruins. This prophecy was fulfilled **centuries after** Micah's prophecy and well after the Dead Sea Scroll copies of Micah were written. Samaria remained a flourishing city until about A.D. 250—800 years after the prophecy was written, and 400 years after Micah's prophecy was copied in the Dead Sea Scrolls! But if we were to visit ancient Samaria today, we would see grapevines growing in the deserted ruins, evidence for the extremely detailed accuracy of the biblical prophecies.

C. THE SEQUENCE OF ANCIENT EMPIRES

1. **Daniel 2**: In his interpretation of Nebuchadnezzar's dream, Daniel gave a preview of the sequence of world empires, beginning with Babylon and King Nebuchadnezzar, and then predicting the Persian, Greek and Roman Empires to follow. Read the details of these empires in Daniel 2, as well as in Daniel's vision in chapter 7. **All** these prophecies have been fulfilled exactly as predicted.

2. **Daniel 11** gives an amazing amount of detail about events involving Persia, Greece, Syria, Egypt and Israel. All these events took place subsequent to Daniel's time and many of them were not fulfilled until **after** the Dead Sea Scrolls were copied and hidden. History confirms these prophetic details, which can be checked out in any good historical encyclopedia. This historical confirmation of detailed prophetic accuracy is **very** difficult for the skeptic to refute.

D. THE PROMISE OF THE MESSIAH

Throughout the Old Testament there was an awareness among the Jewish people of a coming, personal Messiah. **Many, many** predictions and details about the ancestors, birth, life and death of the Messiah who was to come were all written down hundreds of years before the time of Jesus, the Messiah. Here are just four:

1. **Ancestry**: He would be human - predicted in Genesis 3:15 with fulfillment recorded in Matthew 1:25. He would be Jewish - predicted in Genesis 22:18 with fulfillment recorded in Matthew 1:1. He would be from the line of Isaac - predicted in Genesis 26:4 with fulfillment recorded in Matthew 1:2. He would be from the line of Judah - predicted in Genesis 49:10 with fulfillment recorded in Luke 3:33. He would be a descendant of King David—predicted in Isaiah 9:6-7 with fulfillment recorded in Matthew 1:1 and 6.

2. **Birth**: He would be born in Bethlehem - predicted in Micah 5:2 with fulfillment recorded in Luke 2:1-7.

3. **Life**: He would have a "messenger" go before Him - predicted in Malachi 3:1 with fulfillment recorded in Mark 1:1-8. He would have a healing and teaching ministry—predicted in Isaiah 35:4-6 and 61:1-2 with fulfillment recorded in Matthew 9:35 and 11:2-6, as well as the other Gospels.

4. **Death**: Predictions of detailed events surrounding His death such as: He was scourged and spit upon (Isaiah 50:6) and mocked (Psalm 22:6-8); they gambled for His garment (Psalm 22:18); His death was with criminals (Isaiah 53:12); He was given sour wine to drink (Psalm 69:21); His side was pierced (Zechariah 12:10); His bones were not broken (Psalm 34:20). Other details of His death by crucifixion (which was an unknown form of execution in Old Testament times) are given in Psalm 22:6-8, 16, 18 and Isaiah 53:5, and the fulfillment is recorded in the four Gospels.

In addition, a detailed time frame for the coming of the Messiah (and the End Times) is outlined in Daniel 9. Even the most radical critic is forced to acknowledge that a straightforward reading of and calculations from Daniel 9:25-26 lead to the crucifixion of Jesus of Nazareth in the 1st century A.D.

The fact that so many predictions of the coming Messiah were fulfilled in Jesus Christ can only be explained in one way—that the Old Testament prophets were inspired by God. These prophecies which match the facts of the ancestry, life and death of Jesus cannot be denied, no matter how hard the skeptics try. And prophecies concerning His death by Roman crucifixion cannot be manipulated or artificially fulfilled.

The possibility that any one person could fulfill these predictions of the Jewish Messiah just "by chance" are so small that we can't even comprehend such an improbability. Here's an illustration that helps us to understand how slim the statistical chances are: Imagine a **huge** ball of sand, the radius of which is from here to the nearest star (not the sun). Consider more than 400 of those balls. Now take one grain of sand, paint it red and hide it in one of those huge balls of sand. What are the chances that someone, blindfolded, could find that one red grain of sand hidden in one of those 400+ immense balls—on the first try, just by chance? **No chance!** The amazingly accurate predictions about the life of Jesus Christ are beyond chance—they are supernatural!

E. THE PREDICTION OF CHRISTIANITY

1. Malachi 1:11— "For from the rising of the sun even to its setting, My name will be great among the nations . . ." (NASB).

This prophecy will be completely fulfilled when the Lord returns and establishes His kingdom, but even now Christianity is a foreshadowing and a partial fulfillment of this prophecy. Think of it! The Name of the **GOD of Israel** is known and worshiped worldwide today—everywhere that Christianity has spread!

2. John 8:12 and John 9:5— "I am the light of the world."

Throughout the years since this statement was made, the message of Jesus Christ has brought enlightenment and advances in education, medicine, charities, etc.

3. Matthew 24:35— "My words will by no means pass away."

Not only have the words of Jesus not passed away, they have spread worldwide.

4. Matthew 16:18— "I will build My Church, and the gates of Hades shall not prevail against it."

This prophecy has come true.

5. Acts 1:8 - "You shall be witnesses to Me . . . to the end of the earth."

In the past 2000 years this prediction has certainly been fulfilled as Christian missionaries have spread the good news of Jesus Christ around the world.

At first glance these prophecies may not seem like powerful Christian evidence, but think it through. No matter what position the skeptic takes concerning the predictions of Christianity, the prophecies have come true, and the skeptic must admit that they were made and written down at a time when Christianity seemed about to be snuffed out by the pagan Roman Empire.

CONCLUSION

Fulfilled prophecy is very powerful evidence for the reliability of the Bible. When it can be shown with hard evidence from history that detailed prophecies found in ancient manuscripts were fulfilled hundreds of years later, just as predicted, the skeptic has a hard time trying to explain away the evidence. The clear and convincing evidence of fulfilled prophecy testifies to the accuracy—and thus the reliability—of the Bible.

❖   ❖   ❖

CHAPTER FOUR

DOES GOD EXIST?

Is there any solid proof for God's existence? In the past almost everyone believed that God existed, but these days many people openly doubt or deny that there is a God. The existence of God remains a basic, fundamental question in the minds of many people, and the answer to this question is of utmost importance.

According to the Bible, God has given mankind sufficient evidence of Himself so that no "**blind** leap of faith" is necessary. In fact, Romans 1:20 states that the evidence for the existence of God is so overwhelming and clear that an individual has no excuse for not believing in God. The Bible says that anyone who turns away from the evidence and denies the existence of God is a "fool" (Psalm 14:1 and Psalm 53:1).

Where is this indisputable evidence that the God of the Bible really exists? It is all around us in nature! God has revealed Himself to all peoples all over the earth through nature. The natural world all around us cries out for an explanation of its existence, and the only adequate explanation is God.

As we continue our study of Christian Evidences with evidence for the existence of God, some of the terms in the next two chapters may be unfamiliar and the concepts may seem difficult to understand. If you carefully study and think through these chapters, you'll gain a good grasp of this important subject, evidence for God's existence. However, if you become discouraged as you study Chapters 4 and 5, skip to Chapter 6 and continue from there. You can return to Chapters 4 and 5 later.

In this chapter the word "argument" is used frequently. Just as lawyers present "arguments" to support a case in court, so in this chapter the word "argument" means "a way of reasoning or logical deduction."

The evidences for God that we find in nature are called the "Naturalistic Arguments for the Existence of God." The naturalistic arguments are known as the Cosmological Argument, the Teleological Argument, the Anthropological Argument, and the Ontological Argument for the existence of God. You might think that these arguments are highly complex and complicated because of their long and technical-sounding names. However, they are really quite simple and easy to follow once the basic "Law of Cause and Effect" (or the "Causal Argument") is understood. We will return to them after we have covered the "Law of Cause and Effect".

A. THE LAW OF CAUSE AND EFFECT

Let's start with the Law of Cause and Effect (the Causal Argument). There are three basic steps in the Law of Cause and Effect:

1. Step One: For every *effect* there must be a *cause*.

Nothing can exist or be produced without a cause. There must be a cause behind every single thing that exists and every event that happens. If something exists or happens (an effect), there must be an explanation for how it came into being or happened (a cause).

> *Example 1*: The Automobile
> When we see a new car (effect), we know there was something that caused this effect—namely, a car manufacturer (cause). The car did not just materialize out of thin air or suddenly appear by chance from piles of steel, plastic, wires and rubber!
> *Example 2*: The Universe
> Both scientific evidence and philosophical reasoning show that at a certain point the universe began to exist. Since the universe (the effect) exists, there must have been a cause that brought it into being.

2. Step Two: No *effect* can be greater than its *cause*.

The cause must always be equal to, or greater than, the effect it causes.

A large tree falling over must have a cause behind it that is greater than a gentle breeze. The cause must be **greater in quantity**. A beautiful painting of a landscape must be caused by something greater than a few cans of paint falling over on a canvas. The cause must be **greater in quality**.

Example 1: The Automobile
A car manufacturer (cause) is greater than an individual car (effect). The factory with its raw materials and machines and assembly lines which produced the car is superior quantitatively (in measure) than the car. In addition, the intelligence behind the design and programming of the car is superior qualitatively (in excellence) than the car itself.

Example 2: The Universe
The universe (effect) must have had a cause that is both qualitatively and quantitatively greater than, or superior to, the universe itself.

3. Step Three: There *must* be a first *cause*.

Behind every immediate cause there is obviously a chain of prior causes. Take this page, for example. Behind this printed page is a cause— a printing press. But what caused the printing press, and what caused the cause of the printing press, etc., etc.?

Example 1: The Automobile
The car comes from a long chain of causes involving designers, car concepts, factories, architects and contractors who built the automobile assembly plants, cement factories, steel mills, rubber factories, etc. But at some point there was a beginning to that car's chain of causes, because we know that the chain of causes for cars doesn't stretch back eternally!

Example 2: The Universe
In explaining the existence of the universe, we logically conclude that there must either be a chain of causes stretching back into infinity, or there must have been a first cause that got everything started, including time. Since scientific evidence indicates that the space-matter-time universe had a definite beginning, there must be a first cause that brought it into being. And if we think this through logically, that first cause must itself be **infinite** and **eternally uncaused** and **self-existent**.

4. The Bible

The Bible states that the First Cause of everything that exists is **God**, who is greater than all the effects. Hebrews 3:4 says, "Every house [the effect] is built by someone [the cause], but He who built all things is God [the First Cause]." While this concept requires faith (Hebrews 11:3 and 6), it does not require any more "faith" than to believe that the universe is eternal or that it came about by itself!

Conclusion

The logical conclusion of the Law of Cause and Effect is that behind everything there is either an infinite and eternal chain of greater and greater causes, or there is ultimately a first great Cause (which is itself infinite and eternally uncaused). The Christian takes a **reasonable** step of faith at this point and believes that the God of the Bible is this infinite and eternal First Cause.

B. FOUR "CAUSE AND EFFECT" ARGUMENTS FROM NATURE

There are four lines of reasoning, known as the Naturalistic Arguments for the existence of God, which present evidence from nature for the existence of God. All four arguments from nature are based on the Law of Cause and Effect, or the Causal Argument. When the Causal Argument is applied to the matter and motion of the universe, it is called the **Cosmological Argument**. When applied to the design and order found throughout the universe, it is called the **Teleological Argument**. When applied to the immaterial aspects of man, such as his ability to think rationally, make moral judgments, and appreciate beauty, it is called the **Anthropological Argument**. And when applied to the concept of a "Supreme Being" it is called the **Ontological Argument**. Let's trace each of these arguments for the existence of God in a little more detail.

1. The Matter and Motion of the Universe: The Cosmological Argument

a. Definition

The term "cosmological" comes from the Greek word, "cosmos," which refers to the universe as an orderly system. The Cosmological Argument for the existence of God applies the Law of Cause and Effect to the matter and motion of the universe, or cosmos.

b. The Argument

Matter:
The matter (or material) of the universe exists—it is an effect. The Law of Cause and Effect demands a cause for the material of this universe. Where did the original "stuff" come from? How did it all get started? There must be an adequate cause for all the stars and planets, as well as every single atom and subatomic particle that exists. Did the universe create itself—or is there a First Cause, that is, a Prime Maker?

Motion:
The motion of the universe is an effect. There must be an adequate explanation for the cause of all the intricate movements in this universe, from orbiting electrons to reverse spinning moons to spiraling galaxies and everything in between. Did the motion start by itself, or is there a First Cause, that is, a Prime Mover who began the complex motion of the universe?

c. The Bible

Only the Bible gives a completely adequate and rational answer to the question of "how it all got started." The Bible tells us that "The heavens declare the glory of God; and the firmament shows His handiwork" (Psalm 19:1). "For by Him all things were created that are in heaven and that are on earth, visible and invisible . . . all things were created through Him and for Him. And He is before all things, and in Him all things consist" (Colossians 1:16-17). "For since the creation of the world His invisible attributes are clearly seen, being understood by the things that are made, even His eternal power and Godhead" (Romans 1:20). See also Genesis 1:1; Psalm 33:6, 9; Hebrews 11:3.

d. Conclusion

The only adequate, rational, commonsense answer to the origin of the matter and motion of the universe is the answer of Romans 1:20: God and

His eternal power. The matter and motion of the universe argue logically and powerfully for the existence of God.

2. Design and Purpose in the Universe: The Teleological Argument

a. Definition

The term "teleological" comes from the Greek word *telos*, which means "a purposeful end," and refers to the design and "purpose" in nature. The Teleological Argument applies the Causal Argument to the design and order in the universe.

b. The Argument

Design:
Is there design in our universe? Think of the structure of the atom, or the DNA molecule, or the marvelous design of the human eye. Consider the amazing variety of the forms of life around us, both plant and animal. Each one is a miracle of structure and function, specifically designed for the part it plays in the world. How did these design specifications arise? Is it possible that all this intricate design (effect) came about by chance (cause)? The Law of Cause and Effect demands that each of these effects must have a cause that is greater quantitatively and qualitatively.

Order:
Is there order in the universe? Think of the involved and delicate balance of nature in our world. Consider the many natural laws that govern the universe—the law of gravity, for example, and the orderly orbits of the planets in our solar system. How did the "instructions" for the intricate laws of nature get "programmed"? Could all the order (effect) we see in nature and in the universe have somehow begun by chance (cause)?

Example: The well-known "Watchmaker Argument" - Suppose we were hiking through a desert, and we suddenly found a beautifully designed and crafted Swiss watch, ticking away in the middle of the desert. What would we conclude? That some grains of sand had just happened to come together by lucky chance, and somehow formed a watch? Of course not! We would **logically** conclude that the beautiful watch (effect) was designed and created (or caused) by a skillful watchmaker! The incredible effects of order, structure and design in the universe demand an **intelligent** cause—a Designer.

c. The Bible

Psalm 94:9 gives the Teleological Argument from Scripture: "He who planted the ear, shall He not hear? He who formed the eye, shall He not see?" Romans 1:20 states that God's divine nature is stamped in many ways on the design and structure of His creation. Think of how our heavenly Father's care, for example, is imaged in the parental care that we see in the animal kingdom. Think of how God's revelation of Himself as a triune God is reflected in the space-matter-time universe He created. God is one in substance or essence, yet He is three in Persons—a trinity or "tri-unity." The universe, as a tri-unity of space, matter and time, mirrors the divine nature of its Designer.

d. Conclusion

Have you ever watched a spider spin a web? Is it even conceivable that this highly complex creature with its "web spinner" and its "web know-how" could have come about by chance? Think of the human brain. How can we explain the development of such a complex computer, the capacity of which is never fully utilized by any individual? Certainly not through evolution! The theory of evolution cannot explain the fact that the human brain "developed" **beyond** what is needed for the "fittest to survive." Surely the wisdom of the Designer that is stamped all over this orderly universe is evidence of the existence of the God of the Bible.

3. The "Human" Qualities of Mankind: The Anthropological Argument

a. Definition

The term "anthropological" comes from the Greek word "anthropos," which means man or mankind. In the Anthropological Argument for the existence of God the many different non-material aspects of mankind—the rational, moral, aesthetic, volitional and spiritual qualities—are considered as effects and then the Causal Argument is applied.

b. The Argument

Rational Qualities
Applying the Causal Argument, the fact that people can reason and think is an effect. The cause of this effect must therefore be rational and able to think.

Moral Qualities
Mankind is moral. Cultures all over the world have moral regulations. In every culture, certain things are designated as "right" and certain things are designated as "wrong." Morality in mankind is an effect; the cause must also be moral. Could the moral quality in mankind have evolved by chance?

Aesthetic Qualities
The fact that people can appreciate beauty, truth and goodness is an effect. Therefore the cause of this effect must be able to appreciate beauty, truth and goodness. Could these human qualities have evolved by chance?

Volitional Qualities
The fact that people have the capacity to make decisions and choices is an effect. You cannot get "will power" from a stone or a tree! The cause of volitional capacity must have a will. The Cause must be volitional.

Spiritual Qualities
The fact that human beings are spiritual beings, with the ability and capacity to love and worship, demands that the cause be spiritual as well. Could human spirituality have just "happened"—by chance?

c. The Bible

"So God created man in His own image" (Genesis 1:27). "For since the creation of the world His invisible attributes are clearly seen, being understood by the things that are made . . ." (Romans 1:20).

d. Conclusion

Romans 1:20 declares that God's nature can be seen in what He has made. As we think through the ultimate cause of the many different non-material aspects (effects) that we see in humankind, we realize that we are led to a character description of the God of the Bible! The First Cause **must** be rational, aesthetic, volitional and spiritual, just as the Bible indicates. To say that all these effects in mankind have come into being without God is to deny the Causal Argument and to opt for the idea that they all came about through a **chance**-guided rearrangement of molecules and matter! Morals, for example, are not molecular structures! And even if it could be shown (which it cannot!) that the non-material aspects of mankind were chance molecular arrangements, then there would be no ultimate meaning to any of these aspects. The skeptic could never say it is "wrong" to steal his money if there are no ultimate moral standards and morality only happened by "chance." The critics would have to admit that even the validity of their reasoning and arguments against God carry no weight if they are consistent in their position that rational thought came about by chance! Rational thought and morality and the other non-material aspects of man are **irrefutable** arguments for the existence of God.

4. The Concept of a "Supreme Being": The Ontological Argument

a. Definition

The term "ontological" comes from the Greek word, "ontos", which means "to be," or "to exist." The Ontological Argument is the most philosophical of the naturalistic arguments for the existence of God, and can be difficult to grasp in its formal statement. It is easier to understand, however, when we apply the Causal Argument to the idea of existence.

b. The Argument

Mankind seems to have an idea or concept of a "most perfect being." This idea or concept is an effect. The cause must be greater. The fact that the mind of man can conceive of a "most perfect being" demands that the cause must be greater than the concept. Carried to its logical conclusion, the fact that people can conceive the idea of a most perfect Being is evidence that there **is** a most perfect Being, who is the ultimate Cause of the idea of the most perfect being. In other words, there is only one thing greater, qualitatively and quantitatively, than a mind that can conceive the most perfect idea of the most perfect being—and that is the most perfect

Being itself! Therefore, the most perfect being must exist. This Most Perfect Being must be the God of the Bible.

c. The Bible

"For in Him we live and move and have our being, as also some of your own poets have said, 'For we also are His offspring.' Therefore since we are the offspring of God, we ought not to think that the Divine Nature is like gold or silver or stone, something shaped by art and man's devising" (Acts 17:28-29). In these verses, Paul appears to have assumed the ontological argument as he debated with the philosophers in Athens. If we live and move and even think about God, then it stands to reason that the cause of these effects must be greater than silver or stone. In fact, the only cause great enough would be the God of the Bible that Paul was proclaiming.

d. Conclusion

Although the ontological argument is difficult to follow, it is a valid and strong philosophical argument for the existence of God. In fact, some of the greatest unbelieving thinkers of human history have acknowledged this as the most powerful argument for the existence of God.

CONCLUSION

The naturalistic arguments which God has made intrinsic and essential to His work of creation are **so obvious** that His word of revelation (the Bible) declares that those who will not believe are **without excuse** (Romans 1:20). Furthermore, they are "fools" for not being open to the evidence. "The fool has said in his heart, There is no God'" (Psalm 14:1 and 53:1).

❖   ❖   ❖

CHAPTER FIVE

ARE THERE OBJECTIONS TO THE EVIDENCE THAT GOD EXISTS?

This chapter will help you know how to answer some of the typical questions or objections which may be raised about the arguments for the existence of God which were discussed in Chapter 4. Additional helpful information on God as the Creator can be found in Chapters 9, 10 and 11. Emphasize to the questioner that the answers you are giving are the most **reasonable** and **logical** options.

A. COSMOLOGICAL ARGUMENT

1. Objection: Who created God?

> **Answer**: No one created God. God is the "First Cause." If anyone asks you this question, go through the Causal Argument from Chapter 4. Show the person that, **logically**, there must either be an eternal "chain of causes" or an infinite "First Cause." The most reasonable and logical option is that there was a First Cause. It takes as much— *or more*—faith to believe that the universe is eternal than to believe in an infinite and eternal, uncaused "First Cause."

2. Objection: What's the scientific evidence?

> **Answer**: An unbeliever **must** (logically) choose to believe that either

the universe is **eternal** or it was **created**, because of the scientific "First Law of Thermodynamics." This law (which is known by every high school student taking General Science) states that energy can change in **form** but not in **quantity**. That is, the amount of energy within the universe is constant, even though it can vary in form.

For example, when we put gasoline in our cars, the chemical energy of the fuel is converted into different forms of energy: motion, heat and noise. But no energy is lost and no energy is gained—it is just changed in form. Einstein's famous equation, $E=Mc^2$ (Energy = mass multiplied by the speed of light squared) shows that all the matter in the universe may be equated with energy. This energy may take various forms, but no energy is now being created or destroyed. What does this Law say about the origin of the material universe? It shows, logically, that the universe could not have created itself—either it is eternal (has always existed) or it had a beginning. These are the only two **rational** options.

The "Big Bang" theory of the origin of the universe currently prevails in the scientific community. This theory does not answer the logical question of where the original mass-energy came from. The Big Bang theory holds that the whole universe began 15-20 billion years ago as a very dense "dot" of mass-energy which exploded and has been expanding ever since. There are many scientific problems with the Big Bang theory, but the biggest is the problem of **where the original mass-energy came from**. Believing the Big Bang theory actually takes more faith than believing that the earth was created.

Although the First Law of Thermodynamics seems to leave the door open for either of the above two options, the Second Law of Thermodynamics indicates that the universe is **not** eternal, but had a beginning. The Second Law states that there is always a tendency toward disorder and decay in this universe. Living things die, machinery wears out, buildings crumble, stars burn up.

Yes, there are "events" of increasing order, such as the building of an automobile on an assembly line or the development of an unborn child in the womb. These examples might **seem** to contradict the Second Law of Thermodynamics, but that is because these examples are **not** "closed systems." They are "open systems" where "outside help" is being given to them. (In these examples the "outside help" is auto assembly line workers or a developing baby's mother.) These examples illustrate small "pockets" of increasing order within a larger closed system (the universe) of decreasing order. The overall tendency in the universe is toward disorder and dis-integration. Our sun is burning up and cannot last forever. Without "out-side help," the universe will eventually run down. (By the way, the Bible has a lot to say about "Outside Help" for our universe!)

Because of the Second Law of Thermodynamics, then, it reasonably and logically follows that at some point in the past the universe was more ordered than it is today. In fact, the Second Law **strongly** implies that there was a beginning to this universe—it is **not** eternal, and it must have been created.

The First and Second Laws of Thermodynamics are solid scientific statements. These Laws **demand** a beginning and a Creator for this uni-verse. Far-out ideas, such as an eternally cyclic universe (which would not require a beginning) are futile "cop-outs" to get around the **proven laws** of Thermodynamics.

The late Carl Sagan, a well-known non-Christian scientist, wrote, "The cosmos is all that is, or ever was, or ever will be." Carl Sagan **chose** to believe that there is no First Cause (God), even though it is **not more scientific** to believe that the "cosmos is all that is." Because there is **no** real evidence for Sagan's idea of an "eternal cosmos," it actually takes more faith to believe in an "eternal cosmos" than to believe that the God of the Bible is the First Cause. Many non-Christians, however, choose to believe the idea of an "eternal cosmos" or to believe that everything came about from nothing via some kind of a "Big Bang!" Why? The real reason is not based on evidence but rather to avoid having to acknowledge that there is a God!

The first verse of the Bible permits only one possibility: "In the begin-ning God created the heavens and the earth" (Genesis 1:1). The New Tes-tament states the case for creation very clearly: "By faith we understand that the worlds were framed by the word of God, so that the things which are seen were not made of things which are visible" (Hebrews 11:3).

B. TELEOLOGICAL ARGUMENT

1. Objection: I believe that the natural development of the universe re-sulted, over many years, in design and order. I think that if we place the date of the "Big Bang" far enough in the past, over long periods of time natural laws would develop to bring about design and order.

First Answer: First, use the cosmological argument (see Chapter 4).

The cosmological argument must be answered **first**! You can use this answer with anyone, even if you don't know a lot of "heavy" science! Just keep asking, "But **how** did it all get started in the first place? **Where** did it all come from? Remember cause and effect. What was the first cause? Where did the so-called very dense microdot of mass-energy come from? **When** did it get started?" What started the "Big Bang?"

 Second Answer: Second, tell the questioner that scientific evidence rules out this objection. Scientifically, you **cannot** demonstrate that design and order will develop if you have more time—in fact just the opposite will result. The more time you have, the more **disordered** things become! The proven Second Law of Thermodynamics states that in any closed system, disorder **increases**. The universe is naturally a closed system, and things are becoming **more disordered**— design and order are **not** increasing.

The only "exceptions" to this Law occur when there is "outside help." Use the example of a baby developing in the womb—the baby is increasing in order, but only because it has "outside help"—the mother. If the "system of the developing baby" is cut off from that "outside help," the baby will die. Without outside help, the universe itself will eventually die of disorder and decay—because of the Second Law. Remember that the Second Law of Thermodynamics is a proven scientific fact.

Christians know that in the future God will reach into our universe and bring "outside help" into our disordered world and bring about a "new heavens and a new earth." But right now the Second Law is in operation and the overall tendency is **not** toward increased design and order, but toward decay and disorder.

2. Objection: I don't see order and design in the world around me—I see only chaos, disintegration and death! I deny the teleological argument!

Answer: Yes, there **is** a lot of chaos and disorder around us. The Second Law of Thermodynamics tells us why this is true. Things **are** running down, decaying and burning up. But the orderly natural Laws are still operating. And we can still observe many, many magnificent examples of overwhelming and complex design, such as in the atom, the DNA molecule, or the human eye.

3. Objection: I admit that there is design and order in life forms, but I believe that all order and design came about through evolution, not through a "Creator God."

Note: Before you start to answer this objection, think through a basic definition of evolution. At present, the theory of evolution describes the development of life as a process by which lower, less complex forms of life result in higher, more complex forms of life over many years and many generations. Selected mutations (changes), which occur entirely by chance, supposedly cause beneficial changes in a species, allowing the fittest to survive and pass along the new trait to future generations. (For more detail on creation and evolution, see Chapters 9, 10 and 11.)

First Answer: Ask the objector to **show you the evidence** for the evolutionary process! You should know the following points:

a. Evidence for evolution has **not** been demonstrated in the **laboratory**.

i. Life has never been produced in the laboratory. Even if life is ever produced in a laboratory, it will not occur by chance—it will be produced by intelligent scientists, under very closely **controlled conditions!**

ii. Mutations are random changes in the genetic codes of the DNA molecule. Generally, mutations are destructive, rather than beneficial. In laboratory radiation experiments with fruit flies, for example, only harmful mutations occur, not beneficial mutations. In fact, if any "beneficial" mutations occur, there is an overall loss of information to the species.

Even evolutionary scientists agree that evolution has not been demonstrated in the laboratory. For sample quotes on this subject, see the last page of Chapter 11, "Did God use Evolution or Progressive Creation?"

iii. Don't confuse **genetic variation** with evolution. Hybridized flowers, fruits and vegetables, selective breeding of cattle or new breeds of dogs are examples of genetic variation, **not evolution** (although some people try to call this "micro-evolution"). Breeders are working with a gene pool that's **already there!** No **new** genetic information has been added. In just about every high school science textbook you will read about the celebrated case of England's light and dark peppered moths. This is a case of genetic variation—not evolution!

The theory of evolution claims that all changes came about purely by "chance." "Survival of the fittest" and natural adaptation to the environment do operate, but this is **not** evolution. It is genetic variation at work in nature. No *new* **genetic information is being added** to the already existing gene pool.

b. Evidence for evolution is **not found** in the **fossil record**.

No "transitional forms" are found in the fossil record. Transitional form fossils would be fossils of organisms which are in the process of changing from one species to another species. The fossil record shows a **sudden** appearance of invertebrates, and there are **no** transitional forms between invertebrates and vertebrates (animals with skeletons), or between one form of vertebrate and another form of vertebrate. The late Stephen J. Gould, evolutionist and professor of paleontology at Harvard University wrote, "Concerning the fossil record . . . we have sought to **impose** a pattern that we **hoped to find** in a world that **does not really display it**" (emphasis added). For quotes by other evolutionists concerning the fossil record, see Chapter 11.

Example: Evolution theorizes that birds evolved from reptiles, but there are **no** transitional fossils, such as reptiles with scales changing to feathers or forelimbs changing to wings. It has now been shown that the highly touted archaeopteryx fossil, which evolutionists claimed was a transition between reptiles and birds, is not a transitional form at all—it's just an extinct bird! Evolutionary scientist W. E. Swinton, of the British Museum of Natural History, makes this unequivocal statement: "There is no fossil evidence of the stages through which the remarkable change from reptile to bird was achieved." (See Chapter 11 for this reference.) Furthermore, fully formed birds have been found in the fossil record in rock layers that are lower than layers containing dinosaur fossils.

The biblical record of creation contradicts the evolutionary assumption that reptiles preceded birds. Genesis 1 states that birds (Day 5) were created **before** reptiles (Day 6)! "Theistic evolution" theorizes that God used evolution to form the universe and everything in it, but theistic evolution is difficult, if not impossible, to fit into the biblical creation account. (See also Exodus 20:11 and Mark 10:6.)

Second Answer: Explain to the objector that if order and design came about through evolution, then **all** design and order we see in nature **must** be explained by evolution. How the evolution of the most complex species and the most complex biological mechanisms came about by chance must be explained!

Consider the development of the spiders' web-spinning machinery or the metamorphosis of a caterpillar to a butterfly. How could these (and many other) amazing phenomena in nature develop by chance—from nothing—and the species manage to survive during the many generations needed to evolve the many essential and complex biochemical mechanisms involved? Many organisms are irreducibly complex—that is, like the mousetrap, **all** parts must be developed at the **same time** for the organism to function properly. One part without the others is useless!

Furthermore, consider the human brain or the human eye. How could these incredibly complex organs develop by spontaneous, chance mutations from a one-celled organism? Even Charles Darwin, the "father of evolution," acknowledged the difficulties in explaining how complicated organs could have come about. In *The Origin of Species*, Darwin wrote, "To suppose that the eye with all its inimitable contrivances . . . could have been formed by natural selection, seems, I freely confess, absurd in the highest degree."

George Wald, professor of biology at Harvard University, admits in the secular scientific journal *Scientific American*: "Most modern biologists, having reviewed the downfall of the spontaneous generation hypothesis [evolution], yet unwilling to accept the alternative belief in special creation, are left with nothing."

C. ANTHROPOLOGICAL ARGUMENT

1. Objection: I don't agree that humans are rational or moral. I believe that the process of rational thought is only a physico-chemical function of the brain, and morality is only societal training and conditioning.

Answer: You're inconsistent! If mankind is not rational, you would not even be able to debate the existence of God with me, as you're attempting to do!

Sociological evidence shows that human beings have a "built-in sense" of "right and wrong." Mankind is **innately** moral. Although the moral conscience of people can be hardened and distorted, it is still evident.

Example: Murdering children or stealing someone else's wife are viewed as "wrong" by people all over the world, in every culture. This fact demonstrates that "morality" is a "built-in" feature of mankind. Even the cultures that are far removed from biblical moral standards reflect a God-given moral conscience. "For when Gentiles, who do not have the law, by nature do the things contained in the law . . . who show the work of the law written in their hearts, their conscience also bearing witness . . ." (Romans 2:14-15).

2. Objection: I agree that humans are rational and moral beings, but I think that evolution produced humans as rational, moral beings.

  Answer: Starting with the evolutionary assumptions, ask the questioner, "If everything that exists came about by chance, **when** and **how** did 'chance' produce morality?" How can you 'inject' morality or reason into a collection of molecules that came together by **chance**, no matter how complex it is? We don't expect morality from the complex arrangement of molecules that we call a computer. So how, and at what point in the evolutionary process, did humans acquire morality (since you believe that humans are really only a more complex collection of molecules than a computer)?

  Furthermore, tell the objector: Even if it were possible to show that rational thought and morality came about through a chance rearrangement of molecules (evolution), then thought is not really "rational," and moral values are essentially meaningless, because they only happened by chance! Furthermore, if moral values came about by chance through evolution, then the objector should not be angry if you steal his car or destroy his house—or even kill his pet—because you are just "rearranging" the molecules! So, if thought came about by chance there can be no **truly** rational thought, and if moral values came about by chance there are no **absolute** moral standards. You cannot get morals from molecules!

  Continue to press the questioner for an answer, because **apart from God, there is no logical answer!**

CONCLUSION

Maybe you had a hard time understanding some of the unfamiliar scientific terms and information in the last two chapters. Go over the material again and it will become more clear. Whether or not these chapters were difficult, it is important to realize the following fact: in the "battle" between those who believe there is a God and those who deny the existence of God, as far as the evidence goes, we have the "heavy artillery" and **they** have only "pea-shooters"! People who choose to believe otherwise do not realize the amount of evidence for the existence of God, or they intentionally ignore the evidence. **By far, the greater body of evidence is on** "God's side."

The important thing to remember is that apart from God, there are **no logical answers** to explain the existence or the complexity of the universe, the existence and diversity of the things we see about us in nature, or the existence of human qualities such as rational and moral thought. The Bible makes the point very succinctly: "The **fool** has said in his heart, 'There is no God'" (Psalm 14:1).

❖ ❖ ❖

CHAPTER SIX

IS JESUS GOD?

If Jesus was not more than a good man, He was a mad man or a bad man! Does this make sense to you? Although it sounds controversial, and maybe even heretical, it is sound logic and makes perfectly good sense. In fact, we Christians should be able to present this logic to the typical non-Christian who says that Jesus was a good man, but only a man. Jesus claimed to be God, so either Jesus was who He claimed to be or He was not a good man at all. If He was not God, then He deliberately deceived many people—or else He was deceived Himself! In fact, if Jesus was not God, He is still deceiving millions of people who are staking their eternal destiny on Him. But Jesus is more than a good man—He is LORD! Let's see if we can build a solid case with good evidence for this logical conclusion.

As you study this chapter, look at the chart below. It illustrates the different choices people make about Jesus and the logical paths they must follow to reach their conclusions. Choosing to believe false information about Jesus leads to incorrect conclusions about who He is, but believing the true information leads to the logical conclusion that JESUS IS LORD! It's important to follow the chart throughout the entire chapter.

LEGEND
LEADER
LUNATIC
LIAR
LORD

There are only five possible rational choices a person can make when confronted with the claims of Christ. What are they?

JESUS CHRIST—LOGICALLY LORD

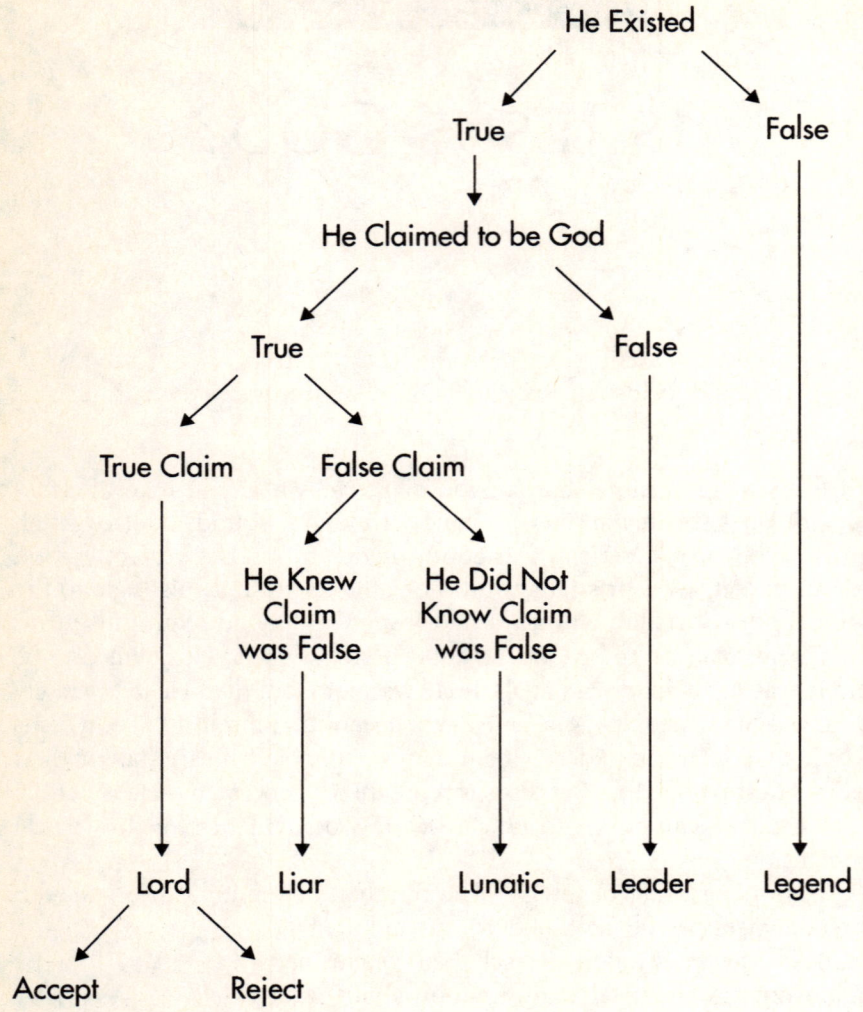

(Based on a chart from *Evidence Demands a Verdict,* Josh McDowell, published by Campus Crusade for Christ © 1972, 1979.)

A. JESUS CHRIST WAS ONLY A LEGEND

Very few people believe that Jesus Christ is only a "legend." There's just too much evidence for His existence. Most people, even non-Christians, realize that there is plenty of evidence that Jesus of Nazareth was a real historical person. Encyclopedias and history books accept and record His life as historical fact. Although the **exact** dates of His birth and death are not precisely known, there is **no** doubt about His historical existence. Four authors of New Testament books record the life of Jesus, and many early Christian writings also document His life. In addition, non-Christian writers

> **LEGEND**
> LEADER
> LUNATIC
> LIAR
> LORD

of the 1st century mention Jesus as a person who truly existed. Here are a few examples of evidence from **non-Christian** writers of the late 1st and early 2nd centuries:

1. **Tacitus**, a Roman historian, wrote that when Nero heard that the citizens suspected him of starting the great fire of Rome in A.D. 64, "to suppress the rumor, he falsely charged with the guilt, and punished with the most exquisite tortures, the persons commonly called Christians . . . Christus the founder of the name, was put to death by Pontius Pilate in the reign of Tiberius" (Annals, XV. 44), about 100 A.D.

2. **Suetonius**, also a Roman historian, mentions "followers of Chrestus . . ." (Life of Claudius, 25.4), about 120 A.D. (Chrestus is a different spelling of "Christ.")

3. **Pliny the Younger**, a Roman governor of Bithynia (112 A.D.) wrote to the emperor Trajan, saying that he had tried to make Christians bow down to the statue of the emperor Trajan "and to curse Christ, which a genuine Christian cannot be induced to do . . . They affirmed . . . that they were in the habit of meeting on a certain fixed day before it was light, when they sang a hymn to Christ as to a god, and bound themselves to a solemn oath, not to do any wicked deeds, but never to commit any fraud, theft, adultery, never to falsify their word . . ." (Epistles, X.96).

4. **Josephus Flavius**, a Jewish historian, wrote: ". . . Jesus, a wise man, if it be lawful to call him a man, for he was a doer of wonderful works, a

READY TO GIVE AN ANSWER

teacher of such men as received the truth . . . He drew over to him many of the Jews and many of the Gentiles. He was the Christ, and when Pilate, at the suggestion of the principal men among us, had condemned him to the cross, those who loved him at the first did not forsake him . . ." (Antiquities, xviii.33), written early in the second century.

5. The **Talmud** and other early writings of Jewish Rabbis did not deny that Jesus lived—nor did they deny that He did miracles! He is mentioned as Yeshua of Nazareth. (Yeshua is the Hebrew word for Jesus.)

Conclusion: Historical evidence supports the existence of Jesus of Nazareth, a Jew who lived in Israel in the 1st century. In ancient times even the opponents of Christianity never doubted the historicity of Jesus. The conclusion that Jesus is just a legend is not a reasonable option. The historical evidence is too overwhelming.

B. JESUS CHRIST WAS ONLY A GREAT HUMAN LEADER

On the chart, follow the "False" arrow under "He Claimed to be God." This arrow designates people who believe that Jesus existed, and that He was an extraordinary human being, a great moral teacher and human "Leader" who lived a life of selfless service, but that He never *really* performed miracles and never *actually* claimed to be God.

How do people come to this conclusion? A number of years ago some religious scholars decided to try to "discover" the "real" historical Jesus, who, they claimed, was not God. Most of these scholars believed that God is **not** the ultimate Author of the Bible. They asserted that the Bible was merely the "words of **mankind** about God," not the "Word of **God** to man." In their view, the Bible contains human errors, and the authors of the Gospels exaggerated many of the stories when

LEGEND
LEADER
LUNATIC
LIAR
LORD

they wrote about the life of Jesus. These religious scholars believed that the "real" Jesus of history was a good man and a great moral and ethical teacher, but not God! They suggested that Christians could find the "real" Jesus by picking and choosing the ethical sayings and "good neighborly" deeds of Jesus and treating only those selections as historical events. They regarded the rest of the record as non-historical "exaggerations" added by the early Christians. Many people still follow this line of thinking today.

In fact, the "Jesus Seminar" is a group of "theologians" who have actually voted on which actions and words of Jesus they think are true and acceptable, and which are fictional! When the news media report the "findings" of this seminar, many people blindly accept the results as fact.

The biggest problem with this line of thinking is that solid evidence has shown the biblical documents to be very reliable, as we saw in our first three chapters. In addition, the time gap between the life of Jesus and the earliest written New Testament documents is now known to be quite short, probably less than 20 years. The Gospels were written within the life span of the people who knew and saw Jesus, both believers and unbelievers. It's inconceivable that the early Christians could have deceived so many people who knew Jesus into believing that He did miracles, if He didn't! And if Jesus had not claimed to be God, these people could and would have accused the authors of putting words into the mouth of Jesus and writing exaggerated tales about Him. However, as far back as we can trace in historical literature, no one ever challenged the historicity of the claims Jesus made, as recorded in the gospel record.

Jesus made some radical statements about His own deity. In fact, His claims to be the Messiah, the Son of God, (which the skeptics reject) are often interwoven with His great moral and ethical teachings (which skeptical people accept as true and noble sayings!) It's unreasonable and extremely biased to try to fracture or separate these Scriptures. In addition, the Gospel writers wrote that not only did Jesus claim to be God, but that the Jewish leaders understood His claim and tried to kill Him for blasphemy (lying about God). The following passages are examples:

John 5:18— "Therefore the Jews sought all the more to kill Him, because He . . . said that God was His Father, making Himself equal with God"

John 8:58-59— "Jesus said to them, 'Most assuredly, I say to you, before Abraham was, I AM.' Then they took up stones to throw at Him; but Jesus hid Himself and went out of the temple . . ."

Here Jesus not only claimed eternal existence but also ascribed to Himself the holy Name of God: "I AM"!

John 10:30— "I and My Father are one"

After Jesus said this, the Jewish leaders attempted to kill Him. Their explanation: ". . . because You, being a Man, make Yourself God" (10:33).

Matthew 26:63-65— ". . . The high priest answered and said to Him, 'I adjure You by the living God that You tell us if You are the Christ, the Son of God.' Jesus said to him,' It is as you said' . . . Then the high priest tore his clothes, saying, 'He has spoken blasphemy!'"

Luke 22:70— "Then they all said, 'Are You then the Son of God?' And He said to them, 'You rightly say that I am.'"

John 19:7— "The Jews answered him [Pilate], 'We have a law, and according to our law He ought to die, because He made Himself the Son of God.'"

Conclusion: The Gospel biographies which document the life of Jesus clearly state that Jesus claimed to be God. Unbelieving Jewish leaders also recognized that He claimed to be God. They did not demand that He be crucified because He taught, "Love your neighbor as yourself"!

Every person must decide whether Jesus' claim to be God was a true claim or a false claim. People who choose to believe that Jesus never claimed to be God reject the historical evidence. They think they can follow the life and teachings of the human leader Jesus, without all the consequences of acknowledging Jesus as LORD. Sadly, against all the evidence, they choose to place their religious faith in an empty, powerless, false "Jesus," who was just another "good human ethical teacher," but not God, and not Savior, and not LORD.

C. JESUS WAS DELUDED, AND ONLY *THOUGHT* HE WAS GOD

On the chart, follow the arrows with those who say "True" to "He Claimed to be God." Then follow the arrow that designates people who believe that Jesus was mistaken and only **thought** He was God.

LEGEND
LEADER
LUNATIC
LIAR
LORD

In his well-known book, *The Quest for the Historical Jesus* (written early in the 20th century), Albert Schweitzer suggested that Jesus really did claim—and really did believe—that He was God and the Messiah of Israel. But, Schweitzer concluded, Jesus **wasn't** God, He only **thought** He was God! Many liberal theologians since Schweitzer's day have gone along with this idea, saying that Jesus was a good moral teacher, but that He was sincerely deluded when

He claimed to be God, and that He didn't realize His mistake until He was on the cross. In Schweitzer's mistaken view, this is why Jesus cried out, "My God, my God, why have you forsaken Me?"

There are at least two problems with this theory. First, if you think you're God when you're not, you're insane! If Jesus suffered from "delusions of grandeur" and wrongly believed Himself to be God, then He was mentally ill! Some deluded people think they are God, but they exhibit unbalanced or schizophrenic behavior patterns. Although some of the Jews thought Jesus was insane because of His claims, others realized that Jesus' character was **not** that of a lunatic (John 10:19-21). When we read the accounts of the life of Jesus, we find that He was an exceptionally stable and balanced person. Crowds of people followed Him to listen to His teachings. Children were attracted to Him. His life certainly didn't resemble the behavior patterns of a person who suffered from delusions!

Second, it is not logical to commit your future and base your life on the teachings of a person you **know** is seriously deluded. If Jesus was mistaken in the area of His deity, perhaps He was confused in **other** areas of His teaching, too. It just doesn't make sense to follow the teachings of someone you **know** to be unstable or deluded. Those who conclude that Jesus was "sincerely deluded," in spite of overwhelming evidence to the contrary, are deluded themselves!

D. JESUS WAS A LIAR

Did Jesus claim to be God, even though He **knew** He was not God? On the chart follow the arrow that designates those who believe that Jesus **knew** His claim to be God was false.

Many Jewish leaders—both then and now—say that Jesus purposely led people astray by falsely claiming to be God. In early rabbinic writings they wrote, "On the eve of Passover they hanged Yeshua [Jesus] (of Nazareth) . . . He hath practiced sorcery and beguiled and led astray Israel" (Babylonia Sanhedrin 43a). The word "sorcerer" probably refers to the charges made by Jewish leaders that the miracles of Jesus were acts of sorcery, and done by the power of Satan (Matthew

LEGEND
LEADER
LUNATIC
LIAR
LORD

12:24, Mark 3:22, Luke 11:15). The statements that "He led the people astray" likely refers to the Jewish leaders' knowledge that Jesus had claimed to be God. You certainly don't lead people astray by teaching people to "love your neighbor as yourself"! The only way that Jesus could have led the people astray, from the Jewish point of view, would have been to make the claim of Deity. The leaders charged that He had deliberately misled people with His false claims (John 19:7).

If the charges made by the Jewish leaders were true, and Jesus **deliberately** made false claims of deity, Jesus was a **liar**! But if Jesus was a liar, He was a most unusual liar! Liars usually show a pattern of lying, but Jesus consistently showed a pattern of truth. Liars are usually selfish and self-serving, but Jesus always served others. Liars lie to protect themselves, but Jesus did just the opposite: He didn't run away to protect Himself, as liars would do. In fact, if Jesus was a liar, He was an incredibly foolish liar, because He died for His "lie"!

Conclusion: Historical evidence shows that Jesus claimed to be God, but people who refuse to recognize that His claim was true are left with only two logical choices: Jesus was a lunatic or He was a liar. Those who believe that Jesus was deluded—that He only **thought** He was God—are forced, logically, to conclude that their "great moral teacher" was actually mentally ill!

If Jesus deliberately made false claims to be God, we must conclude that He was a liar. If He was a liar, He was **not** a "good, moral leader" who gave great ethical teachings. In fact, if He was a liar He was a very **bad** man who has led millions of people astray.

All the evidence that we have of Jesus indicates that He did not exhibit the characteristics of a lunatic or a liar. Most people realize that these are not logical or reasonable options. Only the hard-nosed skeptic takes such options.

E. JESUS DID CLAIM TO BE GOD AND HIS CLAIM WAS TRUE!

LEGEND
LEADER
LUNATIC
LIAR
LORD

If you have followed the logic and evidence in this chapter, using the chart as a visual aid to show how the evidence does not permit the Legend, Leader, Lunatic or Liar options, you will agree that the only truly **logical** conclusion is that Jesus **did** claim to be God, that His claim was **true**, and He is **much, much more** than just a great human religious leader! He is **God** and He is **Lord**!

CONCLUSION

In his book, *Mere Christianity*, C. S. Lewis, one of the greatest thinkers of our time, wrote ". . . he really foolish thing that people often say about Him: 'I'm ready to accept Jesus as a great moral teacher, but I don't accept His claim to be God.' That is the one thing we must **not** say. A man who was merely a man, and said the sort of things that Jesus said, would **not** be a great moral teacher. Either this man was, and is, the Son of God, or else a madman or something worse . . . but let us not come with any nonsense about His being a great human teacher. He has not left that option open to us . . . This man we are talking about either was (and is) just what He said, or else He is a lunatic or something worse. Now it seems obvious to me that He was neither a lunatic nor a fiend, and, consequently, however strange or unlikely it may seem, I have to accept the view that He was, and is, God."

The evidence in this chapter should lead an honest observer to the logical conclusion that Jesus is God, and worthy of being called **Lord**. Once people have recognized that Jesus is God and logically Lord, however, they must make a final decision—whether or not to trust in Jesus as their personal Savior and acknowledge Him as Lord over their lives (see Romans 10:9). Satan and his followers, the fallen angels, know that Jesus is Lord (James 2:19), but they refuse to bow to Him as Lord. Unfortunately many people also make a deliberate decision to reject Jesus and turn away from Jesus Christ, the Lord (Matthew 7:13). As we end this chapter, the important question each one of us must ask ourselves is: "Have I personally put my trust in Jesus Christ, the Son of God, as my Savior and have I acknowledged Him as Lord over my life?"

CHAPTER SEVEN

❖ ❖ ❖

MIRACLES OR MYTHS?

A. DOCTRINE OF MIRACLES

A short and concise statement of the biblical doctrine of miracles is found in Mark 10:27: "with God all things are possible." Miracles really happen! Miracles are powerful evidence that we have a God who is supreme over all the earth and over any false gods, a God who acts on behalf of His people. Believers should **expect** miracles to be included in the Bible.

B. DENIAL OF MIRACLES

Many people, even some Christians, seem to be embarrassed or ashamed of miracles and want to explain them some other way. They try to explain away the miracle of Creation week as "God did it through evolution." They deny the miracle of the crossing of the Red Sea, saying "They walked through a shallow, marshy area." The miracle of Jonah's rescue is interpreted as "just an Old Testament parable"—or, can you believe—"A boat named 'Big Fish' rescued Jonah from the sea!"

As we learned in our last chapter, some people attempt to explain the miracles of Jesus by proposing that His followers exaggerated the ordinary deeds of a good moral leader after His death. For example, they try to explain the miracle of Jesus walking on water by saying that "the disciples thought He was walking on the water—but He really was walking on a sandbar!" Some critics of the Bible venture to say that the miracle of the feeding of the 5,000 was accomplished by the disciples hiding loaves of bread in caves and then passing it out to the Lord under their robes so it "appeared" that a miracle had taken place! Others say the miracle occurred when Jesus gave a sermon about sharing, and everyone got out their lunch bags and shared their barley loaves and fish with one another. The over-zealous believers reported it as miraculous, and before long people believed and wrote that Jesus had actually multiplied bread and fish. People who attempt to explain miracles away don't seem to realize that if the miracles of the Bible are untrue, Christianity is in big trouble! Remember, the miracle of the resurrection of Christ is **essential** to the Christian faith. If the miracles of the Bible are really only myths, we are left with an unreliable Bible that is filled with legends, exaggerations and outright lies. On what, then, can we rely?

C. DEFINITION OF MIRACLES

Miracles are not just "things that happen which we can't explain"! A miracle is an extraordinary event in the physical world which takes place when the supernatural realm breaks into the natural realm and **temporarily** interrupts or changes the **ordinary** course of events. God is in control over His creation at all times. A divine miracle is simply a deviation from God's normal and natural way of working.

A model train layout is a good illustration. Usually the train is allowed to run along on its tracks in its ordinary and usual way, according to the conditions and plan and pattern laid out by the designer of the model train layout. But sometimes, for his own reasons, the designer reaches in to change around some scenery or pick up an engine or boxcar and move it to a different location. In the same way, God, the Great Designer, normally allows His creation to run in its usual and ordinary way, by the natural laws and patterns He set up in the first place. But sometimes, for His own special purposes, God reaches into His creation to work in an unusual way—a miraculous way!

D. DIAGRAM OF MIRACLES

The diagram on the next page shows the Christian world view. The inner circle represents the natural realm, governed by natural laws. A naturalist or secular humanist believes that the natural realm is all that exists. Christians, however, know that there is also a **supernatural** realm, the unseen world, and that there's both a good side and an evil side to the supernatural realm. (See Ephesians 6:12.) Notice that God is outside the circles—because He is the Creator. A miracle occurs when the Designer reaches into the natural realm and temporarily interrupts the natural laws or changes the normal course of events. Notice, also, a small arrow that penetrates from the **evil** supernatural realm. We **should not assume that all miracles are from God**—Satan is the great deceiver! "Black magic" and occult healings are "evil miracles." But God is still in ultimate control and Satan can only do what God allows. (See Job 1-2.)

THE CHRISTIAN WORLD VIEW

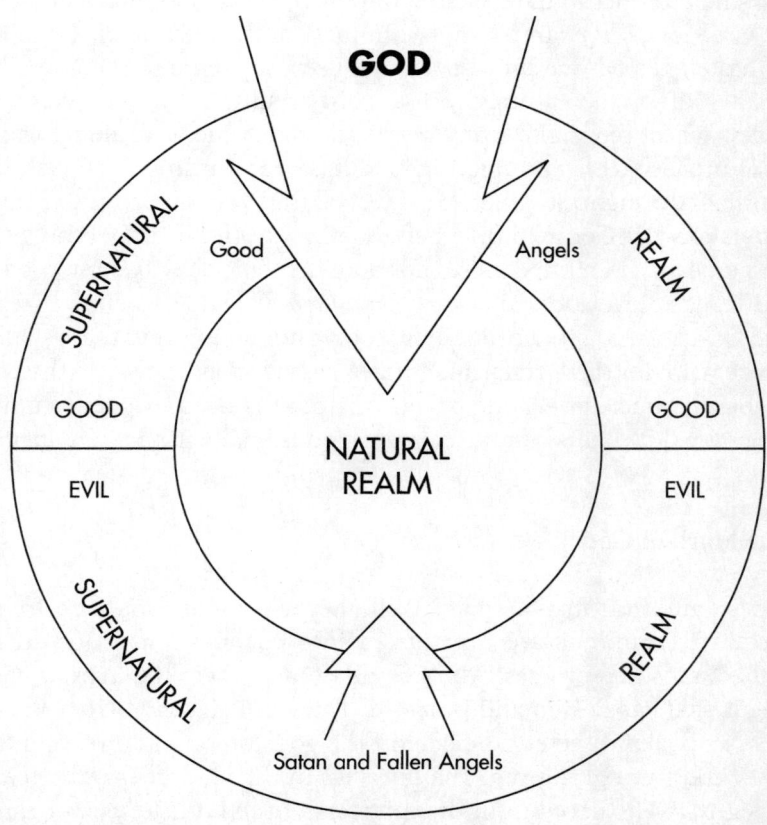

E. DISCUSSION OF MIRACLES

1. The Mechanics of God

How does God perform a miracle? Sometimes He does it by overcoming natural laws. Sometimes He speeds up or slows down natural laws. Sometimes He synchronizes a **natural** event with **His** time schedule. For example, when Israel crossed the Jordan River, God may well have synchronized an earthquake and landslide to cut off the flow of the river so the people could cross over. (See Joshua 3:16.) The walls of Jericho **may** also have fallen because of another earthquake—possibly a major aftershock—which was perfectly timed by God!

In his book, *Miracles,* C. S. Lewis divided the miracles of Jesus into "miracles of the Old Creation," and "miracles of the New Creation." Miracles of the **old creation** are small glimpses of what God **has been doing** since Creation. For example, in the miracle of the feeding of the 5,000, Jesus hastened a natural process that has been happening throughout history. After all, by the natural processes of agriculture God has been turning a few wheat seeds into many grains and much bread all along, and by natural processes of reproduction God has been turning a few fish into many fish throughout time! Miracles of the **new creation** are small glimpses of what God **will do** when the new creation is fully brought in: no more death, no more disease, no more demonic activity, no more natural disasters. Revelation 21:4 says, "And God will wipe away every tear . . . there shall be no more death, nor sorrow, nor crying; and there shall be no more pain, for the former things have passed away." So when the Bible describes a miracle of healing or raising from the dead, we get a glimpse of what it will be like when the new creation is finally ushered in, in all its fullness.

2. The Mark of God

What are God's miracles like? Well, they're certainly not like fairy tale "miracles." Pumpkins are not turned into coaches and frogs do not become handsome princes! All of God's miracles bear the mark of God. Each miracle has **design** and **purpose**. The Ten Plagues of Exodus 7-12 were specifically directed to discredit the gods of Egypt and to confirm God's Word through Moses. The miracles in the wilderness were God's provision for His people. All the miracles of the Lord Jesus were signs which confirmed the truth that He was teaching. The fact that so many spiritual lessons can be drawn from the miracles of Christ is not forced interpretation. The miracles of the Lord not only confirm His deity, but were designed to teach spiritual truths as well.

F. DESCRIPTION OF MIRACLES

1. Miracles—When?

Major miracles, such as the parting of the waters of the Red Sea so that several million people crossed dry-shod (Exodus 14), or the walls of a great city suddenly collapsing (Joshua 6), or ravens delivering meals (1 Kings 17), or 185,000 enemy troops suddenly dying during the night (Isaiah 37:6) didn't take place every day in Bible times, and they don't occur every day today. Major miracles seem to have occurred in "clusters." Creation Week was a great cluster of really major miracles! The Genesis Flood was a year-long major miracle of catastrophic natural events precisely timed by God to accomplish His purposes of judgment. Clusters of major miracles occurred at the time of the Exodus, and at the times of Elijah, Elisha, and Daniel. There was a tremendous cluster of miracle during the life of Jesus Christ, continuing on into the early church period. And there will be many **major** miracles in the End Times. However, long periods of time with only occasional major miracles went by between the clusters of major miracles in the Bible.

The fact that clusters of major miracles appear to have occurred only in biblical times does **not** mean that all miracles have ceased today. God has always been at work in His creation and with His creatures in a

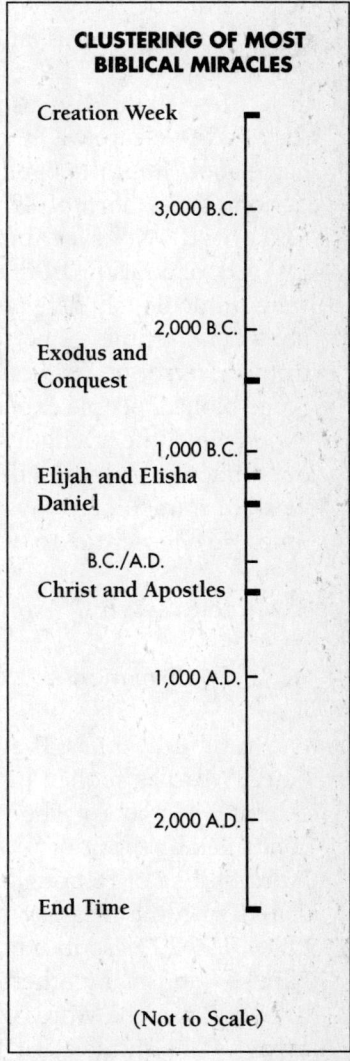

CLUSTERING OF MOST BIBLICAL MIRACLES

Creation Week

3,000 B.C.

2,000 B.C.
Exodus and Conquest

1,000 B.C.
Elijah and Elisha
Daniel

B.C./A.D.
Christ and Apostles

1,000 A.D.

2,000 A.D.

End Time

(Not to Scale)

supernatural way, and He continues to work with His creation and His people in supernatural ways today, even though they may not seem as spectacular and dramatic as the biblical miracles.

2. Miracles —Who?

It's important to realize that not everyone in the Bible performed miracles, and not everyone in the Bible experienced major miracles. Not everyone was a Moses, an Elijah or an Elisha! At the time of Nehemiah, when the people had to rebuild the walls of Jerusalem, they faced a huge task. They could have used some miracles! But no miracles occurred— they had to clear away the rubble and build up those walls by ordinary hard labor! John the Baptist didn't perform **any** miracles, but Jesus said, "among those born of women there is not a greater prophet than John" (Luke 7:28)! Not every biblical character experienced a healing, a famine relieved, or a raising from the dead. Although Daniel and his three friends were miraculously delivered from martyrdom in the fiery furnace or the lion's den, in times of persecution many other believers were not rescued from martyrdom. (See Luke 4:25-27; Mark 6:17-29; 2 Timothy 4:20.) Some biblical people experienced physical miracles; some biblical people experienced the strength of God to endure difficult circumstances without miraculous physical delivery (see Hebrews 11:32-38). God chooses to work in miraculous ways with certain people at certain times. At other times He chooses not to work through miracles.

3. Miracles—Why?

a. Confirmation

In biblical times, the primary purpose for miracles was to **confirm God's Word** as spoken by the people who did the miracles—not **just** to exhibit God's power. The Word of the Lord to Pharaoh through Moses was confirmed by the miraculous plagues. The fire from heaven confirmed the Word of the Lord through Elijah in 1 Kings 18. Many miracles were associated with the message of Jesus, who was the ultimate **Word of God**. Luke 7:16-22 describes how the miracles of Jesus confirmed to John the Baptist—and many others—that Jesus was the Messiah, who **spoke** and **lived** and **was** the Word of God. The apostle John tells us that he recorded many of the miracles of Jesus "that you may believe that Jesus is the

Christ, the Son of God, and that believing you may have life in His name" (John 20:30-31). Hebrews 2:3-4 states that our salvation "which at the first began to be spoken by the Lord, and was confirmed to us by those who heard Him, God also bearing witness both with signs and wonders, with various miracles . . ." The miracles showed that the Lord was supreme and His supernatural display of power was a confirmation of His supernatural spoken words. 2 Corinthians 12:12 says that "the signs of an apostle [a messenger of God] were accomplished among you . . . in signs and wonders and mighty deeds." The miracles that occurred during the early days of Christianity confirmed that the message of the apostles was truly God's Word.

b. Illustration

Another important purpose for biblical miracles is to **illustrate and teach spiritual lessons**. Biblical miracles were not just random "magical" acts to make a big splash. They were pre-planned and designed by God to teach spiritual lessons. For example, one of the miracles of Elisha (2 Kings 4:38-41) teaches us that harmful and poisonous things may be mixed in what looks like good spiritual food. Just look at how poisonous books may be mistaken for spiritual food when they're mixed in with good books on the shelves of all too many Christian bookstores! As another example, think of the wonderful spiritual lessons about salvation that we have in the miracle of the healing of Naaman (2 Kings 5). In the miracles of Christ, the blind man who was healed in stages (Mark 8) dramatizes the process of God working with us to lead us to spiritual maturity: learning to follow, learning humility, learning to look up, and learning to let the Lord keep His hands on our lives. The miracle of multiplying the loaves and fish (Matthew 14, Mark 6, Luke 9, John 6) teaches us to bring what we have to the Lord—even if we think it's not much—and He will bless it and multiply it for the glory of God and the blessing of many people. And the Lord used the "negative" miracle of the cursing of the fig tree (Matthew 21:18-22) to teach that people who are busy with only external, outward religious fervor and activity ("glossy religious leaves") are in serious peril! The majority of people in the nation of Israel at that time (represented by the fig tree—see Hosea 9:10 and Luke 13:6-9) were guilty of merely "going through the motions" of worship. Their religious activity was external only, not the result of a love for God. Only those people who produce genuine spiritual fruit are acceptable to God.

G. DECLINE OF MIRACLES

Do miracles still happen today? If the primary purpose of miracles was to confirm the Word of the Lord, should we expect major miracles today, now that the **written** Word of the Lord (the Bible) is complete? As the books of the New Testament were completed, the cluster of major miracles of apostolic days began to decline or taper off. In Christianity's early days even the **shadow** of Peter brought healing (Acts 5:15). Philip was physically transported by the Spirit to another location (Acts 8:39). Dorcas and Eutychus were raised from the dead (Acts 9:36-42 and 20:9-12). Handkerchiefs that had been touched by Paul brought healing (Acts 19:11-12). But by the time Paul wrote to Timothy and Titus (about A.D. 65) or the time of John's epistles (about A.D. 85), it appears that the number of major miracles was starting to decline.

Down through church history, major miracles like those that occurred in the early days of the church have not recurred. Why? Is it that Christians have less faith? No! One reason is that we now have the **written** Bible, so we don't need miracles to confirm the spoken Word of God. In the story of the rich man and Lazarus in Luke 16, the rich man asked if someone could return from the dead (a miraculous event) to warn his brothers about the place of punishment. Abraham replied that the man's brothers had the Law and the Prophets (the Old Testament, the **written** Word of God), so there was **no need** for a miraculous event. The rich man's brothers could and should receive all the information and warning they needed by heeding the messages in God's **written Word**.

However, God is certainly doing miracles today. A miracle occurs every time a person becomes a Christian! Miracles of healing, protection and guidance occur every day through the power of God. But **major miracles** performed by God through the **agency of people** are generally not common today, although it would be wrong to "limit God" by saying that He cannot or would not perform miracles in this way today. For example, in countries where the Bible has not yet been translated into the common language, God may confirm the word of Christian missionaries in dramatic ways.

Christians need to be cautious about miracles done through the agency of people who claim to be operating in the name of Jesus. Jesus Himself warned that some people who do miraculous things in His name really do not belong to Him at all! "Many will say to Me in that day [the final judgment], 'LORD, LORD, have we not prophesied in Your name, cast out demons in Your name, and done many wonders in Your name?' And then I will declare to them, 'I never knew you; depart from Me . . . '" (Matthew 7:22-23). Notice that the Lord does not say that these people didn't really do miracles. In fact they **did** do miracles, but the power behind the miracles was not from God!

CONCLUSION

Miracles are extraordinary events which are a temporary deviation from God's normal and ordinary way of working in the natural world. When God used human agents to perform miracles, their primary purpose was to confirm the word of the Lord as it was spoken through the individual. The more dramatic miracles seem to have tapered off as the written Word of God was completed. Miracles are recorded in the Bible so we will be thankful that we have the supreme and powerful God as our Father, so we will be encouraged to depend on Him, so we can read how God confirmed the teaching of doctrine, and so we can learn the spiritual lessons which the miracles were designed to teach. In our next chapter we will study the greatest miracle, the resurrection of Jesus Christ!

❖   ❖   ❖

CHAPTER EIGHT

IS JESUS ALIVE?

The resurrection of Jesus Christ is the greatest miracle of all, and the truth of the resurrection is absolutely essential to the Christian faith. In fact, according to 1 Corinthians 15, the Christian faith stands or falls on the truth of the resurrection of Jesus Christ! Is there evidence that Jesus Christ really rose from the dead? Yes—there's plenty of excellent evidence! Many skeptics who tried to disprove the resurrection actually became Christians when they started to look seriously and honestly at the evidence.

A. EVIDENCE FROM THE BIBLE

When people who doubt the resurrection ask, "What evidence do you have?" you can say, "Well, I have the reliable reports of at least three eyewitnesses—Matthew, Mark and John!" And don't let the skeptic say, "Oh, you're only using the Bible!" We have already established that the Bible is a reliable historical document—more accurate, in fact, than other ancient books. We can use the biblical records as reliable evidence! As Christians, we accept the biblical record as true because it's the Word of God, but even the unbeliever must acknowledge that the biblical documents are reliable historical documents.

1. Historical Record of the New Testament Documents

a. **Gospels**: The four Gospels give detailed accounts of eyewitnesses of the resurrected Jesus. Eyewitness accounts are important evidence that would be accepted in courts of law today.

b. Acts: The preaching of the Apostles stressed the resurrection, and there is no record that anyone ever came forward to dispute or deny their teaching. See Acts 2:23-24; 4:2; 4:33; 17:31.

c. Epistles: The apostle Paul states that many people saw the risen Christ—on one occasion, over 500 people at once (1 Corinthians 15:3-8)! Many of those eyewitnesses were still alive to corroborate Paul's statement because 1 Corinthians, a letter sent to the Christians at Corinth, was written only about 25 years after the resurrection. When Paul wrote this letter, he knew his readers accepted and believed the resurrection of Jesus without reservation. The letter of 1 Corinthians would never have been accepted as undisputed truth if indeed the resurrection had not taken place.

2. Old Testament Prophecies about the Messiah

All the Old Testament prophecies (predictions) about the Messianic Kingdom assume that the "King Messiah" will live forever. Two examples of Old Testament prophecies about the death and resurrection of the Messiah are the following:

a. Psalm 16: "For You will not leave my soul in Sheol, nor will You allow Your Holy One to see corruption" (Psalm 16:10). Jewish rabbinical tradition believed that this passage was speaking of the Messiah. While preaching to Jews, the apostle Paul used Psalm 16:10 as an example of an Old Testament prophecy which was fulfilled by the resurrection of Jesus, the Messiah (Acts 13:34-37)!

b. Isaiah 53: Isaiah 53 gives a detailed prediction of the death (v 5-8), burial (v 9), **and resurrection** (v 10-12) of the Messiah.

B. EVIDENCE FROM OTHER SOURCES

1. Tradition of the Empty Tomb
Over the past 2,000 years, skeptics have made many attempts to explain away the weight of the tradition of the empty tomb. Some of these attempts are as follows:

a. "Story" explanation

Skeptic: "Christians made up the story—the empty tomb is just a legend."

Answer: These skeptics are ignoring a lot of solid historical evidence. Remember, there were many **non-Christian eyewitnesses** of the crucifixion and burial of Jesus of Nazareth, including Roman soldiers. Probably at least four guards kept watch over the tomb, either Roman soldiers, Jewish Temple Guards, or a combination of both. It was illegal to break the official Roman seal which sealed the tomb, but the men who guarded the tomb reported to Jewish leaders that the tomb was open and empty. Neither the guards nor the Jewish leaders were followers of Christ, so they would certainly have denied a false "story" and produced the body if the tomb was not really empty. How can all these details of the tradition be explained away if the empty tomb is only a legend? The evidence is overwhelming for the fact that there was a tomb where Jesus was buried after His crucifixion, and that it was empty a few days later.

b. "Swoon" explanation

Skeptic: "Jesus didn't really die, He only swooned (temporarily lost consciousness), but later He revived and recovered in the cool tomb."

Answer: The Roman soldiers who were in charge of the execution were all too familiar with death. They would have made sure that Jesus was really dead. In addition, it's absurd to suggest that a man who had been tortured, crucified, pronounced dead and encased in stiff graveclothes could not only survive, but recover sufficiently (without medical treatment) to extricate himself from the graveclothes, get up, single-handedly push aside a one-ton stone, elude a detachment of Roman and/or Temple guards and walk away!

c. "Stolen" explanation

Skeptic: "Jesus' disciples stole His body."

Answer: How could a small group of frightened men pull it off? A heavy, noisy rolling stone closed the mouth of the tomb, which was guarded by Roman soldiers or Jewish Temple Guards (or both) and sealed with an official Roman seal. Would men who ran away in fear when Jesus was arrested suddenly become courageous enough to steal His body from a tomb that was guarded by armed Roman soldiers? Not likely! And how could the disciples have kept a stolen body—and the story—hidden? The authorities certainly had ways to recover stolen property! Furthermore, all but one of the disciples were eventually killed for being followers of Jesus. Would they have been willing to give up their lives when they **knew** that the resurrection was a **hoax**? Not likely!

d. "Slow-witted" explanation
Skeptic: "The followers of Jesus were slow-witted, uneducated peasants, and they went to the wrong tomb!"

Answer: Many intelligent people observed the burial of Jesus in the tomb of a wealthy, well-known Jewish leader. Would **everyone** have gone to the wrong tomb? Surely Joseph of Arimathea would have known the location of his own tomb! The Roman guards and Jewish leaders certainly knew the location of the tomb, and would have quickly and easily produced the body from Joseph's tomb to prevent the followers of Jesus from spreading the "rumor" of the resurrection!

e. "Stoned" explanation
Skeptic: "They hallucinated—they only **thought** they saw a resurrected Jesus Christ!"

Answer: Was the empty tomb a hallucination, too? Why didn't the Jewish leaders stop the rumor that people had seen a risen Christ by producing the body of Jesus? **More than 500 people at one time** (1 Corinthians 15:6) saw the risen Jesus after the resurrection—could they **all** have imagined it?

f. "Spiritual" explanation
Skeptic: "It was a spiritual resurrection—not a bodily resurrection."

Answer: If it was not a bodily resurrection, why didn't the authorities produce the body? Does a "spiritual" resurrection leave graveclothes without a body? Or is this another detail that just happened to "sneak into" the accounts of the resurrection that were **accepted** by eyewitnesses and contemporaries of the writers? Besides, many physical details (Jesus was touched; Jesus ate) were given by the eyewitnesses. All these details must be explained away if the resurrection was only "spiritual."

g. "Something" explanation
Skeptic: "**Something** happened—we don't know what—but certainly not a resurrection, because miracles don't happen!" This is the response of the typical skeptic today.

Answer: The evidence of the empty tomb is **so strong** that some skeptics have to acknowledge that "**something**" happened. All the evidence points to a resurrection, but skeptics will not admit to the possibility of supernatural events, so they come up with the vague explanation that "something" happened—but certainly not a miracle!

h. "Supernatural" explanation

The evidence for the resurrection is so strong that it is very hard for an honest investigator to deny it. The only reasonable explanation for the tradition of the empty tomb (and all its associated details which **must** be explained away if it's not a factual tradition) is that the tomb was **really empty** because Jesus left it by the miracle of the resurrection.

2. Transformation of the Apostles

The disciples of Jesus changed abruptly from a scared bunch of cowards to courageous preachers! All but John died as martyrs. Men who ran away when Jesus was arrested were now willing to die. What caused the change? A stolen body? Not a chance! They changed because they **knew** Jesus Christ was **alive!**

3. Change in Jesus' family

According to the Scriptural record, the family of Jesus went from unbelief (John 7:5) to faith in Him (Acts 1:14) so soon after His death that only a major event—like a resurrection!—would have changed them. James and Jude, the half-brothers of Jesus, wrote books of the New Testament. James became a leader in the Christian church in Jerusalem (Acts 15:13).

4. Conversion of Paul

Saul of Tarsus, the brilliant young Jewish rabbi who was completely convinced that Christianity was a heresy, became Paul, the Christian apostle and a leading proponent of Christianity! This man possessed one of the finest minds in history and was well-versed in the prophecies of the Jewish Scriptures. He became fully convinced that Jesus was the Jewish Messiah, who had risen from the dead! Only an amazing experience can account for such a radical change in such a man. In Acts 9:1-9, Paul tells the story: He **saw** and **heard** the **living** Jesus Christ!

5. Records of the Early Christians

a. **Their Bible**: Early Christians never questioned the accuracy of the historical events and records of the New Testament. There is no evidence that the New Testament records have ever been altered or changed in any way.

b. **Their writings**: Letters, commentaries and written church services all attest to the resurrection. These documents form a continuous overlapping "chain," linking early Christian writings back to the Apostles, who were eyewitnesses of the risen Christ.

c. **Their growth**: The Christian community grew at a phenomenal rate, in spite of severe persecution. Only the strong certainty of the truth of the resurrection could explain this. Not only that, a large number of Jewish priests were among the earliest believers (Acts 6:7). Almost certainly they knew of the "stolen body" tale and they didn't believe it. They believed that Jesus Christ was risen and alive!

d. **Their zeal**: The early Christians were convinced that their message was authentic and vital. Would they have been so excited about spreading the gospel if they suspected it might be a hoax?

e. **Their deaths**: The apostles and many early Christians suffered cruel and agonizing deaths rather than renounce their faith and deny that Jesus was the living LORD. Polycarp, an early Christian leader, knew the apostle John personally and would certainly have questioned John closely about the details and historical accuracy of the resurrection. In 156 A.D. persecution broke out in Polycarp's province. At the age of 86, Polycarp would not renounce his faith in the risen Lord Jesus Christ, crying out in the public arena, "For 86 years I have been His servant and He has never done me wrong. How can I blaspheme the King who saved me?" Polycarp was burned to death for his faith in the risen Jesus Christ.

6. Writings of Josephus

Josephus Flavius was a non-Christian Jewish historian in the first century. In *Antiquities of the Jews*, he wrote the following about Jesus: "He appeared to them [His followers] alive again on the third day, as the divine prophets had foretold. . . ." Critics have tried to suggest that Christians **in-serted** this statement in the writings of Josephus in the 3rd or 4th century AD! However, there is not a shred of evidence to support the idea that the writings of Josephus were "re-worked" and this quote was inserted! Where are the manuscripts that do not have this quotation? All the manuscripts of Josephus contain this quote, including all the early manuscripts which were translated into other languages. The idea that an "insertion" could have been made in all the manuscripts is extremely unlikely!

7. Origin of the Church

The Christian Church was founded on belief in a **living** Lord Jesus Christ, the promised Messiah of the Old Testament Scriptures (Acts 2:22-24). Remember, the earliest Christians were Jews (Acts 6:7), who expected a Messiah who would live forever. They would never have believed in, followed and died for a Messiah who was **dead**!

8. The Christian Ordinances

Baptism portrays the death and **resurrection** of Jesus. "Therefore we were buried with Him through baptism into death that just as Christ was raised from the dead by the glory of the Father, even so we should walk in newness of life" (Romans 6:4). The Lord's Supper, or Communion, is a commemoration of the death of Jesus on our behalf—in view of the fact that He is no longer dead! It is to be celebrated "till He comes" (1 Corinthians 11:26)—and it should be celebrated with joy because Jesus is alive and coming again!

9. Origin of Resurrection Sunday ("Easter")

Although the name "Easter" derives from a pagan Spring festival, the annual celebration of the resurrection day dates back from earliest times to the Sunday following the Jewish Passover. In fact, **every** Sunday is a celebration of the resurrection!

10. Phenomenon of Sunday as the Day for Christian Worship

The earliest Christians were Jewish. They argued about many things—circumcision, the Sabbath laws, feast days, dietary laws—but they never argued about Sunday worship! Jewish people would **never** have begun to worship on any day other than the Sabbath (Saturday) without a major reason. The **only** reason for instituting another day of worship is that the resurrection took place on Sunday, the "first day of the week" (Luke 24:1). Jesus never taught that the day of worship should be changed. His followers started to worship on Sunday to celebrate His resurrection day. Christian worship on **every Sunday since then** (more than 100,000 Sundays!) has been a celebration of the resurrection! The skeptic has a very hard time explaining how Jewish people started worshiping on Sunday, apart from recognizing that a **very** significant event must have taken place on Sunday, the first day of the week.

C. INADMISSIBLE EVIDENCE

1. Visions

For evidence that would stand the test in a court of law, we must have eyewitness testimony of the **bodily** risen Jesus, not "visions." For evidence of the resurrection in this chapter, we didn't even use the vision of John the Apostle in Revelation. However, we did use the testimony (not a "vision") of the apostle Paul. Paul claimed that, as an unbeliever, he had an eyewitness experience (not a vision) of the risen Christ when he was traveling to Damascus to persecute and kill Christians (Acts 9).

2. "Near Death" Experiences

We should be skeptical of reports of "near death" experiences because much of the detail of these so-called "out-of-body" phenomena doesn't line up with Scripture. For example, even unbelievers have experiences of "light" and "joy," yet Hebrews 9:27 emphatically states, "It is appointed for men to die once, but after this the judgment." Furthermore, there is great variation in accounts of "near death" experiences, depending on many factors.

3. The Shroud of Turin

The Shroud of Turin is purported to be the burial shroud of Christ, with an "image of Christ" made by a "radiation scorch" at the time of the resurrection. The Shroud of Turin is probably not authentic because radioactive carbon testing dates the cloth to the Middle Ages (1260 A.D. to 1390 A.D.), and traces of paint have reportedly been found on the Shroud. Even the Roman Catholic Church, which preserves the Shroud in Turin, Italy, has never been completely convinced of its authenticity. However, some authorities claim that the radiocarbon dates are in error because of faulty testing. Furthermore, at present there is no completely satisfactory natural explanation for the image on the Shroud. Further testing will likely be done, but the Shroud of Turin would not be solid evidence for the resurrection of Jesus Christ.

CONCLUSION

As we mentioned at the beginning of this chapter, many skeptics have ended up becoming Christians because of the undeniable evidence for the resurrection of Jesus Christ.

The eminent British philosopher and author, C.S. Lewis, admitted that he was forced to become a Christian **against his will** because he couldn't deny the evidence for the resurrection.

Lew Wallace, the author of *Ben Hur*, started out to write a book disproving the resurrection, but ended up becoming a Christian after investigating the evidence!

Simon Greenleaf was a 19th century Harvard law professor whose legal writings are still used today. He tried to prove that the resurrection never occurred, but became a Christian as he examined the evidence. He then wrote a book entitled *An Examination of the Testimony of the Four Evangelists by the Rules of Evidence Administered in the Courts of Justice*. Simon Greenleaf put the evidence for the resurrection on trial. Verdict: the resurrection won, on the basis of indisputable evidence!

Early in the 20th century, a non-Christian attorney named Frank Morrison was convinced that the resurrection was no more than a "fairy tale ending" to the "Christian legend." He planned to write a book to disprove the resurrection—until he began to examine the evidence himself! He became a Christian and ended up writing a very different book: *Who Moved the Stone?* The first chapter, entitled "The book that refused to be written," is a description of the book he had planned to write before his mind was changed by the evidence for the resurrection!

❖ ❖ ❖

CHAPTER NINE

IS THERE EVIDENCE FOR CREATION?

As we learned in the studies on the existence of God, the universe is either eternal, or it came about from nothing (through time, chance and natural processes)—or it was designed and created by a Designer /Creator. This chapter will present some of the evidence we have for creation and a Creator. There is so much evidence for Creation that we can include only a small amount of it in such a short course! Some of the evidence mentioned in this chapter is scientific and may be difficult to understand. We have given you a suggested reading list at the end of the course if you want more information, or are interested in further reading on this subject.

A. SCRIPTURAL STATEMENTS

Can we use statements from the Bible as evidence for creation? Yes, we certainly can! We have already established with overwhelming evidence that the Bible is a reliable historical document wherever it can be checked out. The statements the Bible makes can—and must—be taken seriously. (See Chapters 1-3 to review evidence for the Bible's reliability).

1. Examples from the Old Testament

The Old Testament begins with this foundational statement: "In the beginning, God created the heavens and the earth" (Genesis 1:1). God created **ex nihilo**—out of nothing! He continued to create throughout six days of the Creation Week, and rested on the seventh day.

Interestingly, if we trace back through history, we find that in most cultures (even pagan cultures), humans measure time by seven-day weeks. There is no **natural** explanation for this practice. 24-hour days, 30-day months, and 365-day years are all measured by the natural rotation and revolution rates, but there is **no** explanation for measuring time by **weeks**—except that God rooted human history in a seven day creation week!

All the Old Testament authors wrote about a Creator. Here are three examples:

Nehemiah 9:6— "You alone are the LORD, You have made heaven, the heaven of heavens, with all their host, the earth and all things on it, the seas and all that is in them."

Psalm 33:6— "By the word of the LORD the heavens were made, and all the host of them [stars] by the breath of His mouth."

Isaiah 45:18— "For thus says the LORD, who created the heavens, who is God, who formed the earth and made it . . . who did not create it in vain, who formed it to be inhabited."

2. Examples from the New Testament

In Mark 10:6, speaking of human beings, Jesus stated, "But from the **beginning** of the **creation** God made them male and female." Jesus didn't believe that human life evolved out of nothing, by time, chance and natural selection! In this passage Jesus clearly implies that God created everything quickly, because He states that human beings were created as male and female at the **beginning** of creation, not after several "geologic ages" of "progressive creation" or millions of years of gradual evolution!

In Acts 17:24 we read, "God, who made the world and everything in it . . . He is the LORD of heaven and earth."

Hebrews 11:3 states, "the worlds [the universe] were framed by the word of God, so that the things which are seen were not made of things which are visible."

B. SCIENTIFIC LAWS: THE LAWS OF THERMODYNAMICS

1. The First Law of Thermodynamics (which we discussed in Chapter 5) is the law of the conservation of energy. The First Law deals with the fact that energy in the universe is constant. No energy is being created or destroyed at the present time—it only changes in form. Since no energy is being created or destroyed, the universe **cannot** have created itself. The Second Law of Thermodynamics shows that the universe **cannot** be eternal. Therefore, it **must** have been **created**.

2. The Second Law of Thermodynamics basically states that the entropy or disorder of the universe is increasing: living things decay and die, stars burn up, etc. The fact that things are running down, burning up and becoming more disordered indicates that there was a time when the universe was more **ordered**. The universe **could not possibly** be eternal, or it would have worn down and burned up long ago. The Second Law demands that there must have been a **beginning**, a time of **greater order**—a creation! (See Chapter 5 for more about this Law.)

3. Creation Comment: There are **no** exceptions to these universally accepted scientific Laws of Thermodynamics. These Laws **clearly** show that the universe **cannot** have created itself out of nothing and the universe cannot be eternal. The evidence leaves us with only one alternative: the universe was **created**!

C. STELLAR SCENARIOS: THE ORIGIN OF THE STARS

1. "Big Bang" Theory

a. The Theory

The "Big Bang" is the present prevailing scientific theory of the origin of the universe. See the diagram below. Very briefly and simply, the "Big Bang" theory suggests that the universe began with a very small, dense, hot "kernel" of cosmic energy, which exploded (with a Big Bang!) 15-20 billion years ago. As temperatures from the explosion cooled and the young universe expanded, clouds of hydrogen and helium atoms slowly formed. From these clouds of gases, stars and the heavier elements were formed about 10 billion years ago. Eventually stars clustered together to form galaxies. Supernovas and "explosions" of aging stars occurred, and the fragments combined to form new stars, such as our sun. Other fragments combined to form planets, including our earth, about 5 billion years ago.

BIG BANG THEORY

Sequence of Supposed Events, from Initial Explosion
to Origin of Solar System and Life

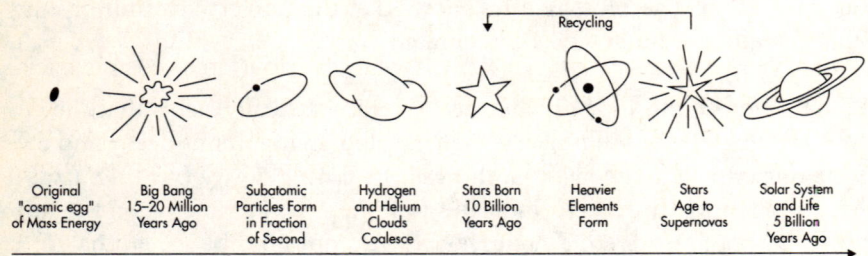

Original "cosmic egg" of Mass Energy	Big Bang 15–20 Million Years Ago	Subatomic Particles Form in Fraction of Second	Hydrogen and Helium Clouds Coalesce	Stars Born 10 Billion Years Ago	Heavier Elements Form	Stars Age to Supernovas	Solar System and Life 5 Billion Years Ago

TIME

b. The Problems

i. Where did the original "kernel of cosmic energy" come from? No reasonable theories have been put forward to answer this question. Remember this is part of the powerful cosmological argument for the existence of God.

ii. What caused the explosion (the Big Bang) of this dense cosmic egg of mass-energy? If this was such an extremely dense kernel of energy, so that even light waves could not escape, an "explosion" is highly unlikely.

iii. If matter went off in all directions following a central explosion, why isn't the universe more homogeneous (uniform) in its distribution of matter? Why aren't the galaxies evenly distributed? Why are there massive clusters of galaxies and "ribbons" of galaxies, with big voids of space between? Why are some distant stars (quasars) too bright and have too much energy? These problems are so great that scientists have had to make up further theories—such as the completely unproven idea of "cold, dark matter"—to account for more gravity.

iv. Why is the universe so "flat"? When things explode, matter goes away from the explosion in all directions! If the universe started with a big bang, the universe should be more spherical.

v. Why do most objects in space have a **circular** motion if everything started from an explosion? And why do some objects (produced from the same explosion) move circularly in **different directions**? Why do Uranus and Venus rotate in the **opposite** direction of the other planets in our solar system? There are 42 moons in our solar system. All of them should revolve around their planets in the same direction, but at least 11 revolve in the opposite direction. Some of the moons revolving around planets have opposite or perpendicular motion to the planet itself! If all matter moved out from a central explosion, there should be more linear motion. All the circular motion and the directional differences in the circular motion is hard to explain apart from creation.

vi. Why is there such a uniform, smooth distribution of cosmic background radiation (CBR), in view of the non-uniformity of the universe? This cosmic background radiation is thought to be left over from the Big Bang, and is still considered to be one of the strongest pieces of supporting evidence of the Big Bang theory. But if it is, why is the CBR so uniform, in view of the non-homogeneity (or non-uniformity) of the supposed expanded universe?

c. "Scientific" Solutions

To date the scientific community has been unsuccessful in answering these problems.

d. Creation Comment

The Biblical account of Creation answers all the questions adequately. Nehemiah 9:6— "You alone are the LORD, You have made . . . the heaven of heavens, with all their host, the earth and all things on it . . ."

2. "Birth of a Star" Theory

a. The Theory

According to the Big Bang theory, stars are "born" as other stars age and are recycled (see diagram).

b. The Problems

i. Contrary to what most people think, the "birth" of a star has never actually been observed. "Infant" stars have been observed (scientists estimate they're about 500,000 years old!) and new stars are "discovered" as more powerful telescopes become available, but the actual "birth" of a star has never been documented.

ii. The idea of the "recycling" of stars may be valid, but it is only a theory. Stars age and burn out, and "black holes" occur as stars run out of energy and collapse in upon themselves, but no complete process of "recycling" has ever been observed.

c. Creation Comment

Genesis 1:14— "God said, 'Let there be lights in the expanse of the heavens . . ." (NASB).

Psalm 8:3— "When I consider Your heavens, the work of Your fingers, the moon and the stars which You have ordained [set in place] . . ."

Isaiah 45:11-12— "Thus says the LORD, the Holy One of Israel . . . My hands stretched out the heavens, and all their [starry] host I have commanded."

The Bible indicates that, right from the beginning, God created differing stars in a fully functional universe. He **created** them as supernovas, "red giants," "white dwarfs," "infant" stars, stars which are different in size and different in **apparent** age. Creating with an "appearance of age" is not deceptive (as some critics suggest) because God Himself **told** us what He did and what to believe! 1 Corinthians 15:41 states, "star differs from another star in glory." And Isaiah 40:26 says, "Lift up your eyes on high, and see who has created these things, who brings out their host by number; He calls them all by name . . ."

D. STONE ANOMALIES: FORMATION AND FEATURES OF GRANITE

There are some very unusual features about the earth's "crustal" rock, granite, that lies underneath the surface sedimentary rocks of the continents. This foundational or "basement" rock is **igneous** rock—rock that once was liquid, but is now solid.

Granite is the most common crustal rock forming the continents. It can sometimes be seen on the surface of the earth, especially in mountainous areas where it has been thrust up through the surface sedimentary rock layers. Sometimes whole mountains are one huge solid hunk of granite, such as El Capitan and Half Dome in California's Yosemite National Park.

1. **Formation of Granite**: Granite is made up of three minerals: quartz, feldspar and mica. These minerals can easily be observed when you look at a piece of granite. Scientists, however, are unable to form true granite in the laboratory—not even a tiny chunk! When granite is heated to the molten state in the laboratory and then cooled down, it is impossible to get granite again—regardless of the time and sequence of the cooling cycle! A granitic lava called rhyolite is obtained. So the granite we see around the earth **could not** have come about, as the Big Bang and evolutionary theory suggest, by molten material slowly cooling down **over a long period of time**. There are other features of granite, such as the interstice-free (no holes) and uniform distribution of the three minerals in the rock which strongly suggest that granite did not form gradually and naturally, but is "creation rock." Even non-Christian scientists who understand phase diagrams appreciate these facts. (A description of phase diagrams is beyond the scope of this course.) At the present time there is still **no** scientifically valid naturalistic explanation for the formation of granite. The evidence points toward a supernatural formation.

2. **Radioactive Halos**: One of the microscopic features of granite is the tiny rings in the mica called "radioactive halos." The presence of polonium microscopic halos strongly indicates that granite had to go from the liquid to the solid state **in less than three minutes!** These halos can only form in solid material and they are formed from the decay of radioactive polonium 218, which has a half-life of less than three minutes. The fact that these polonium 218 rings are formed in solid granite without the associated "radioactive parent rings" cannot be explained naturally. Every indication is that there was polonium (by itself) in the granite right from the beginning. This is further evidence that granite is "**creation rock**," fully formed by God in a very short time—"in the beginning"!

3. **Creation Comment**

Job 38:4— "Where were you when I laid the foundations of the earth?"

Psalm 33:9— "He spoke, and it was done; He commanded, and it stood fast."

Isaiah 45:11-12— "Thus says the LORD . . . 'I have made the earth.'"

Hebrews 11:3— "the worlds were framed by the word of God . . ."

E. STRUCTURAL DESIGNS: PLANNED AND PURPOSEFUL

1. By Time, Chance and Natural Processes?

Time and chance would produce disorder rather than order. Is it likely that a deck of cards thrown from a plane would float to earth and happen to form an orderly design? Would the chances of order be greater if the plane flew higher and more time was allowed for the cards to float to earth? Of course not! (More time, in fact, would produce greater disorder!) What is the likelihood that a chance tornado blowing through a print shop would produce Webster's Unabridged Dictionary? The fact that structural design is found in nature is not evidence for time, chance and "natural processes," but is convincing evidence for creation.

2. By Plan, Purpose and Design!

Structure, purpose and design are evident everywhere in nature. Natural laws and living organisms just don't happen without intelligent direction. Take, for example, the living cell (see diagram on next page). The first evidence for creation is that the cell is **living**! The living cell is like a well-organized and functioning factory. If the person dies, all the essentials of the cells remain, but they are no longer functioning. The mystery of life, itself, needs an explanation and presupposes a Creator.

The existence of DNA is evidence for creation. Inside every cell of every life form is DNA. DNA is a large molecule carrying all the genetic information for the living organism. The DNA in every cell of your body carries the genetic material from your parents. The genetic material in the double helix DNA molecule is composed of four chemical bases. The various and different ways and sequences in which these chemical strands link up directs every function of your body. This is more than just order and structure—this is **information**! Is it likely that this extremely complex sequence, which functions constantly in the microscopic bits of DNA in every single cell of our bodies, could have come about by **chance**?

As an example, think of the game of "Scrabble." If you stacked up all the A's, then all the B's, and on through the alphabet, that would show design. Such order does not come about by chance from a set of Scrabble letters sitting on a table! But when you use the letters to spell words, that's

THE LIVING CELL

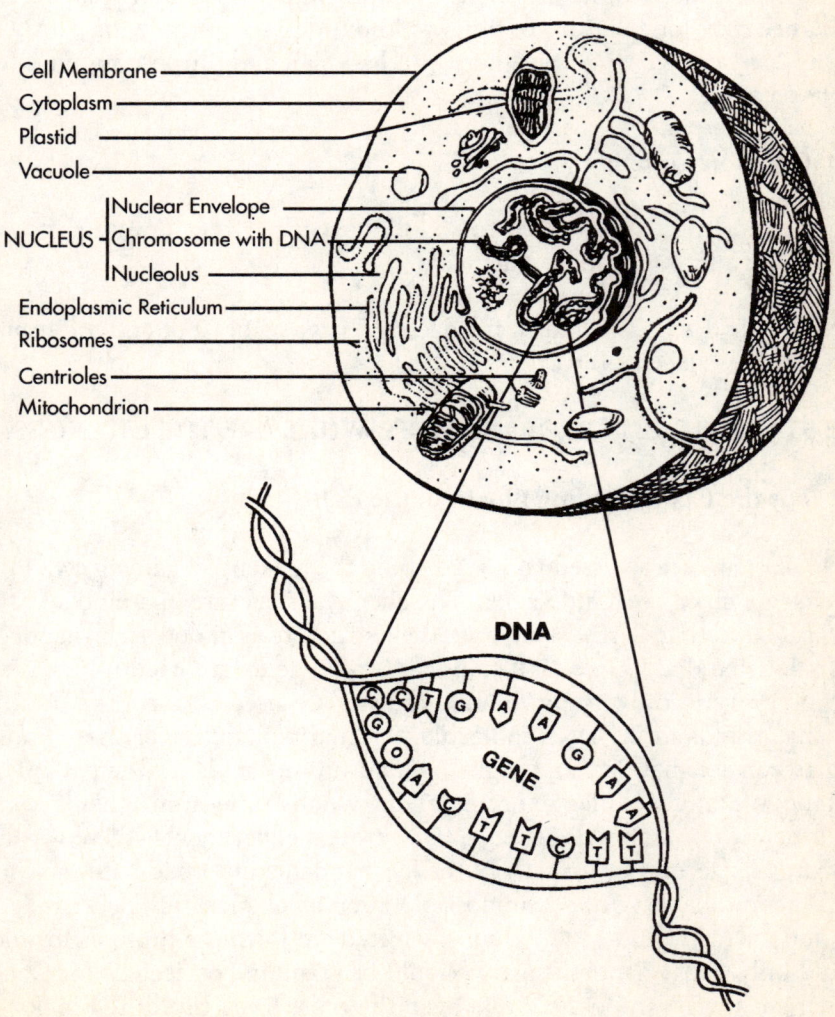

Cell Membrane
Cytoplasm
Plastid
Vacuole
Nuclear Envelope
NUCLEUS — Chromosome with DNA
Nucleolus
Endoplasmic Reticulum
Ribosomes
Centrioles
Mitochondrion

DNA

GENE

more than just order—that's information! And those words didn't come about by chance—an intelligent being planned them!

Another example: compare the four chemical groups that compose DNA to a four letter alphabet. Now, using the four letter alphabet, sit down and write an entire encyclopedia of information on the function of the whole human body—and then make a **functioning** human body out of the information in the encyclopedia! Could such a thing possibly happen apart from intelligent design? Is there the slightest possibility that the incredible complexity of DNA could happen **randomly**—just by **chance** over long periods of time—without design, purpose, or plan? Or was DNA created by **a Designer**, who had plan and purpose in mind for His creation?

3. Creation Comment

Psalm 139:13-14— "For You [God] have formed my inward parts . . . I am fearfully and wonderfully made."

Psalm 19:1— "The heavens declare the glory of God; and the firmament shows His handiwork."

F. STATISTICAL IMPROBABILITIES: WHAT ARE THE CHANCES?

1. For the Basic Building Blocks of the Cell

Proteins are an essential ingredient in the makeup of a living cell. Proteins are chains of amino acids. The chemical structure of amino acids is very interesting. Scientists refer to their structure as either "right-handed" or "left-handed." Only "left-handed" amino acids are used to form life proteins, and only "right-handed" sugars are used to form the double helix strands in the DNA molecule. Ordinary chemistry cannot choose between left-handed and right-handed amino acids and sugars. The famous Stanley Miller experiment in which some amino acids were formed was a highly designed and controlled experiment—there was no "natural selection by chance" of the left-handed amino acids. It is statistically improbable (virtually impossible!) that **by chance** only "left-handed" amino acids would be "randomly selected" to form the proteins for life, and only "right-handed sugars" would be "randomly selected" for DNA! Statistically, it's impossible that even the most **basic building blocks** of protein could be formed by chance and "natural selection." And remember, protein is just **one** of the ingredients of a cell!

There are many more evidences we could examine in just the area of the basic ingredients of the living cell, but as one final example, consider this. Proteins are needed for DNA to operate, but DNA directs the manufacture of proteins—so **both** are necessary for **each** to function, **right from the start**! The **complexity** of the design and interaction of even the most basic ingredients of the cell are clear evidences for creation and a Designer/Creator.

2. For the most Basic Living Cell

What is the likelihood that even the smallest possible living cell would just happen to form by accident? This cell would be composed of 239 protein molecules, each molecule made up of 445 "left-handed" amino acids. The statistical likelihood of the smallest cell just "happening" by chance would be 1 in a 10 followed by **29,345 zeros**! (This huge number is incredibly larger than the diameter of the known universe in inches—that's a 10 followed by only **28** zeros!) It's just not possible!

Statistically, how long would it take? How many **years** would it take, under the **most favorable** conditions, with amino acid combinations taking place every second, to form **just one** cell by chance? This number of years would be **10 followed by 119,841 zeros**—or enough zeros to fill about 60 pages of an average chemistry textbook! (That amount of time makes the 15-20 billion years suggested as the age of the universe to be but a blink of an eye!) Now consider that it would take that incredible number of years to make, by chance, **just the protein part** of the most basic cell—not even the DNA—and certainly not **life**! It's just not possible!

Do statistics like this lead you to believe that time and chance are an adequate explanation for life—or does it seem more likely that life came about from an intelligent, wise and powerful Creator?

3. Creation Comment

Ecclesiastes 11:5— "As you do not know . . . how the bones grow in the womb of her who is with child, so you do not know the works of God who makes all things."

Psalm 139:14 - "I am fearfully and wonderfully made."

CONCLUSION

From *TIME* magazine, December 28, 1992, in an article by Dr. Robert Wright (an non-Christian): "There is more to this universe than meets the eye, something authentically divine about how it all fits together. One intriguing observation . . . is that the universe seems calibrated for life's existence . . . If, at the Big Bang, some basic numbers—the "initial conditions"—had been jiggled, matter and energy would never have coagulated into galaxies, stars, planets or any other platforms stable enough for life as we know it."

Research is driving numbers of scientists to rethink their attitudes toward an Intelligent Designer behind this universe. We Christians do not need to "kiss our brains goodbye" when we believe the information the Bible gives us about the origin of the universe and life upon the earth. "For thus says the LORD . . . who is God, who formed the earth and made it, who has established it . . . who formed it to be inhabited: I am the LORD, and there is no other" (Isaiah 45:18).

❖   ❖   ❖

WHEN DID CREATION TAKE PLACE?

How far back was creation week? Non-Christian scientists (and some Christians) suggest that the Big Bang (their "creation" concept) occurred about 15-20 billion years ago, and they say that the earth is about 4-5 billion years old. In this chapter we will look at the biblical indications of a much younger universe, and discuss some of the evidences from nature that back up the testimony of the Bible.

A. EVIDENCE FROM THE BIBLE

As Christians, we must maintain a high regard for the Bible as the revealed and inspired Word of God. From a straight-forward reading of the Bible we would conclude that the earth and the universe are **not** billions of years old!

1. Creation Week

The records in the Bible give a very short time for creation—just one **week**, not billions of years. "For in six days the Lord made the heavens and the earth, the sea, and all that is in them, and rested on the seventh day. Therefore the Lord blessed the seventh day and hallowed it" (Exodus 20:11).

In Genesis 1 the Bible indicates that right from the start, at the end of the six-day creation week, "the heavens and the earth, the sea and all that is in them" were **mature** and **fully functioning**. The crustal rocks of the earth and moon were created with their various potential radioactive materials already in sequence. The stars were created with their light beams already visible on earth for Adam to see. The trees and plants which God created on the third day of creation week already had rings and were already bearing fruit by the sixth day, when Adam and Eve were created—they didn't have to wait for several years for the trees in the Garden of Eden to mature and produce fruit! The animal kingdom was created ecologically and populationally balanced. Adam and Eve didn't have to learn to walk or talk—it's quite clear that they were created as mature adults, with adult bodies and adult thought processes. Because God created a mature and fully functioning universe, **everything** God made had an **appearance of age**—even though it was brand new. Some critics say that the "appearance of age" in creation seems to be deception on God's part, but they fail to realize that God has **clearly told us** in His Word when and how He created everything. It's right up front—there's no deception! Furthermore, even the most radical unbelieving critic of the Bible must admit to the "appearance of age" concept. It is impossible to conceive of any form of matter without some appearance of age. Try it!

Some people attempt to harmonize the creation account in the Bible with "old earth" scientific theories by trying to stretch out the days of Genesis 1, suggesting that these "days" were actually "geologic ages." They say, for example, that too many things happened on Day 6 for it to have been a literal 24-hour day: Adam was formed; the Garden of Eden was planted by God; Adam named the birds and land mammals; Eve was created. However, this amount of activity is not a problem for **God**! How long would **God** need to create Adam and Eve, or to plant the Garden of Eden? What about Adam naming the animals? We can walk through a zoo in an afternoon, and a zoo contains many more varieties of animals than the animal "kinds" that Adam named in the Garden of Eden. (And remember, Adam in his unfallen state was a lot sharper than we are!)

Nowhere does the Bible support the notion that the days of Genesis 1 were anything other than literal 24-hour days. 2 Peter 3:8 is often presented as a proof that the days of Genesis 1 can be taken as geologic ages. Nothing could be farther from the truth! "With the Lord one day is as a thousand years, and a thousand years as one day," is clearly **not** given as an **equation**, when read properly in the context of the surrounding verses. 2 Peter 3:8 does not mean that the student of Scripture can substitute "a thousand years" or "a million years" or "a geologic age" any place the word "day" appears in Scripture. Such loose hermeneutics (interpretation) allows a person to make the Bible say many things it doesn't teach! Taken in context, 2 Peter 3:8 teaches that **God is not bound by time**. It does **not** teach that the word "day" can mean **any** amount of time.

2. The Genealogies of Genesis 5 and 11

We know that Abraham lived about 2,000 BC. When we add up the years between creation and Abraham's time (given in the family records of Genesis 5 and 11), the creation week appears to have occurred around 4,000 years before Christ. The genealogies of Genesis are **given in years** and thus seem to go in chronological order from father to son. Even if we were to add some years for the possibility of some skipped generations (which is common in biblical genealogies when years are not given), there's no way we could push creation week back more than a few more thousand years. Pushing it back farther would distort the whole biblical chronological framework. The biblical records make our earth and universe very young when compared to the billions of years of the Big Bang/evolution theories!

B. EVIDENCE FROM NATURE

There **are** things about our universe that make it appear old, but that's what we would expect if God created a fully functional universe. Furthermore, God has built into this universe **many** indications that it is a **young** universe. Again, we can only give a few examples in such a brief chapter.

1. Evidence for a Young Universe

a. Evidence from the moon

i. **Craters**— Rock craters on the moon are thought to have been caused by meteor impact early in the moon's history. These craters would have been completely erased if these moon impacts occurred several billion years ago, because lunar rock is subject to flow, and would have leveled out by the present time.

ii. **Radioactivity**— From the Apollo explorations, we know that lunar material is very high in radioactivity. High radioactivity causes heat, so if the moon were really billions of years old it should be intensely hot—but it isn't. Certain radioactive elements or isotopes on the moon have short "half-lives" and should have completely decayed if the moon were 4-5 billion years old—but they are still going strong!

iii. **Distance**— The distance from the earth to the moon is increasing—slowly, but at a steady, measurable rate. If the earth-moon system is 4-5 billion years old, the moon should be much farther from the earth—even if it started in contact with the earth.

iv. **Dust**— The uncompacted dust on the moon is only a few inches deep. Since there is no erosion on the moon, the cosmic dust build-up should be much greater if the moon is 4-5 billion years old. Even counting the cosmic dust which is in the regolith (lunar soil), there should be more cosmic dust if the moon were very old.

b. Evidence from comets

Comets have elliptical, not circular, orbits around the sun. Each time a comet comes close to the sun, some of the comet's material is burned off. This is what constitutes the comet's "tail." Short period comets are those whose orbit around the sun is less than 200 years. If our solar system is really 4-5 billion years old, these short-period comets should all be burned up. But they are still in existence! Even long-period comets should be much smaller than they are. Comets are outstanding evidence of a young universe!

The fact that short-period comets still exist is such a problem for people who believe in a very old universe that scientists devised the theory of "Oort's cloud of comets." This theory postulates that new comets periodically enter the solar system from "Oort's Cloud," to take the place of comets that are being burned up. There is not one shred of evidence for the existence of "Oort's Cloud"—it is only a theory. Another theory suggests that the so-called "Kuiper's Belt," located in the far reaches of the universe, is a source for new comets. This theory faces a similar lack of evidence. And neither theory has a satisfactory mechanism for the perturbing force which is necessary to send the comets into their highly elliptical orbits around the sun.

c. Evidence from the Sun

The higher latitudes of our sun, which is composed of gases, rotate more slowly than the sun's equator. These different rotation rates create friction, which slows rotation. If the sun were billions of years old, friction would have caused it to stop rotating by now. The sun cannot be billions of years old.

d. Evidence from Galaxies

Many galaxies are spiral-shaped, and the galaxies also rotate around a common center—somewhat like a pin-wheel. However, unlike a pin-wheel, the inner stars of a galaxy rotate faster than the outer stars. In other words, the galaxies are "winding up." If the spiral galaxies were really billions of years old, they would be all "wound up" and would no longer have their distinctive spiral shape.

2. "Evidence" for an "Old Earth" Refuted

Again, in this short course we can include only a few examples of the supposed "old earth evidence" and its refutation. See the Reading List for books with more detail.

a. Geologic Column questioned: At least 75% of the earth's exposed surface is sedimentary rock, layers of rock which were formed when sediments settled out of water and then later hardened into rock. Geologists have arranged and named the various rock layers in a sequence, supposedly showing the history of the earth. This is called the "geologic column." Scientists have drawn up a time scale which they have "imposed" on the various layers of the geologic column. (See the diagram below) However, nowhere on earth are all the layers found in the exact sequence proposed by geologists. In some places "older" layers are found over "younger" layers—in fact, at least somewhere on the earth we may find **any** layer of the column on top! How did this arrangement of the geologic column get started? It has to do with the theory of evolution. The rock layers have been dated by the kinds of fossils found in the layers, as determined by where these fossilized life forms are dated by the theory of evolution. In turn, fossils are dated by the rock layers in which they are found. Thus, a **circular** reasoning is used in dating the rock layers! In reality, there are **no**

absolute dates for these layers, and there are significant problems with radiometric dating of rocks (explained in section **b** below).

If the geologic column really represented millions of years of gradual build-up, there should be at least a few meteorites buried in the column—but **not one** has ever been found. The layers of the geologic column are actually evidence for the sediments which were built up rapidly during the world-wide biblical Flood, and the many fossils in the layers are evidence of entrapment and rapid burial during the biblical Flood. (We will study the Flood in Chapter 12.)

b. Rock dating methods questioned: Radiometric dating is used for dating rocks. Radiometric dating involves the decay of radioactive isotopes of elements, through several stages, to a stable condition, which is another known element (such as radioactive uranium decaying to stable lead). If the rates of decay are known, the date of the rock can be calculated by measuring the ratios of the decay products. Radiometric rock-dating methods are not as reliable as the radiocarbon (Carbon-14) method, which is used to date formerly living things. The radiocarbon method has a much shorter half-life than radiometric rock-dating methods, and thus can be calibrated (or checked) by other dating techniques, such as dendro-chronology (counting tree rings). Following are some further problems associated with radiometric rock-dating methods:

i. Scientists make **too many assumptions** about the conditions in the past which lead to the "old" dates that are claimed for rocks. Two examples:

a. Assumptions about **initial conditions**: Radiometric dating methods assume that more of the original element was present than may actually have been present, resulting in an older rock date.

b. Assumptions about **decay rates**: Decay rates may not always have been the same as they are today. Decay rates can be altered by varying conditions. Also, the Second Law of Thermodynamics, which states that things are running down, makes us suspect that decay rates may have decreased with time. Testing which assumes that decay rates in the past are the same as today's rates will result in an older rock date

ii. Rock dates **vary too much**. Sometimes test results from the same rock differ wildly. Volcanic flows of the past 200 years have produced igneous rocks which have been dated as old as several millions of years! Basalt rocks from two lava flows in the Grand Canyon have been dated by radiometric techniques. One flow, buried deep in the Canyon, dated **younger** than the flow near the top of the north rim. This cannot be!

THE STANDARD GEOLOGIC COLUMN AND TIME SCALE
(Based on the Theory of Evolution)

ROCKS	ERAS	PERIODS or EPOCHS	SUPPOSED AGE (in millions of years)	SUPPOSED DEVELOPMENT of LIFE
	CENOZOIC	PLEISTOCENE	1	
		PLIOCENE MIOCENE OLIGOCENE EOCENE	60	HOMINIDS APES MONKEYS
	MESOZOIC	CRETACEOUS	60	PRIMATES WHALES MARSUPIALS MAMMALS
		JURASSIC	180	FLOWERING PLANTS BIRDS
		TRIASSIC	220	DINOSAURS CONIFERS
	PALAEOZOIC	PERMIAN	280	REPTILES
		PENNSYLVANIAN	310	PRIMITIVE REPTILES SWAMP FORESTS (COAL)
		MISSISSIPPIAN	350	AMPHIBIANS
		DEVONIAN	400	SHARKS BONY FISH FERNS
		SILURIAN	450	INSECTS MOSSES
		ORDOVICIAN	500	JAWLESS FISH JELLY FISH
		CAMBRIAN	600	MOLLUSCS SPONGES INVERTEBRATES
	PROTEROZOIC ARCHAEOZOIC	PRECAMBRIAN	3000	BACTERIA ALGAE

(The PENNSYLVANIAN, MISSISSIPPIAN, and DEVONIAN periods are bracketed as CARBONIFEROUS.)

Note: ⅞ths of Earths history is supposedly before the Cambrian Period.

Something is radically wrong with the radiometric rock-dating method!

c. Ice Ages questioned: Old earth proponents state that the earth has been covered with ice several times in its distant past, and millions of years are needed to produce the results that we see, but this can't be proven. There is no doubt that extensive ice action (glaciation) has occurred sometime in the earth's history. However, most of this evidence can easily be explained by water action during the Flood and by the glaciers of **one** "Ice Age" following the Flood. This "Ice Age" was brought on by changes in the climate after the Flood, with much colder climates toward the Poles. The ice would not have covered the whole earth, but glaciers would have built up and extended down from the Poles into Europe, Asia and North America until the carbon dioxide build-up "greenhouse effect" was sufficient enough for the glaciers to recede. The book of Job in the Bible seems to indicate that this "Ice Age" lasted several hundred years after the Flood. Job states: "By the breath of God ice is given, and the broad waters are frozen" (37:10), and "From whose womb comes the ice? and the frost of heaven . . . The waters harden like stone and the surface of the deep is frozen" (38:29-30). How did Job, who lived in the Middle East, know about great expanses of ice? He probably lived not too long after the Flood, and knew of and maybe had even seen glaciers.

d. Fossil coral reefs questioned: Coral consists of the skeletal deposits of marine organisms, which, while living, are organically "glued" together and form a coral reef. At present rates, it takes a long time to form a coral reef. Coral reefs found in the geologic column led scientists to assume that the entire geologic column must be millions of years old. However, closer examination shows that the fossil "reefs" are actually limestone deposits which contain a lot of coral. They are not true reefs. They could have formed relatively quickly by precipitation at the time of the Flood. They are not evidence for an "old earth"!

e. Coal dating questioned: It is assumed that coal beds were formed millions of years ago, and that it took thousands of years for them to form. Yet coal has been made in the laboratory, under the right conditions, in a matter of **days**! The organic matter that was needed for coal to form could have been buried under sediments in the catastrophic worldwide Flood. Fossils of leaves, ferns, tree trunks and marine life have been found in coal beds, indicating rapid burial and compression. Boulders have been found in coal beds, indicating rapid water movement in the formation of coal. Even some human artifacts have been found in coal layers, indicating rapid formation in the not-too-distant past.

3. Evidence for a Young Earth

There are many, many evidences to show that the earth is young, that it couldn't possibly be billions of years old! The earth's core is still too hot; pressures in oil and gas reserves are still too high; too little helium exists in the earth's atmosphere; there's no evidence of 4-5 billion years accumulation of meteoritic dust on the land or in seas; the average of only 7-8 inches of top soil around the earth is too low; erosion of the continents (even with uplift) would have leveled out the earth millions of years ago; the depth of sediment build-up in river deltas and on the ocean floors is far too small. These are just a few of the evidences that point to an earth that is only thousands, not billions, of years old.

Below are some examples of other evidences for a young earth:

a. **Evidence from the earth's magnetic field**: This is one of the strongest and most undeniable evidences there is for a young earth. The earth is a magnet and therefore it has a magnetic "field" around it. Over the last 150 years, accurate measurements of the earth's magnetic field have been made worldwide. These measurements show that the magnetic field is steadily decreasing. At the rate of decrease, the **maximum age** of the earth could only be about 10,000 years. If the earth were billions of years old, the heat from the original electric currents in the earth (which are needed to generate a magnetic field) would have been far too great for the earth to exist. A 4-5 billion-year-old earth is absolutely impossible. Furthermore, there is no known mechanism to either start the original magnetic field of the earth, or build it up again once it has decayed. Thus, theories of a cycling magnetic field have no scientific foundation. The earth's magnetic field strongly indicates **recent creation**.

b. **Evidence from Radioactive Carbon tests**: These tests can be used to date things that contain organic matter—wood, bone, coal, cloth, oil, natural gas, etc. If some organic material remains in a fossil, it can also be dated by radioactive carbon to determine if any radioactivity remains. Anything older than 50,000 years, for example, should show absolutely **no** radioactivity because of the relatively short half life of radioactive carbon (5,700 years). Thousands of radioactive carbon tests have been performed on items such as fossils (including dinosaur bones) or wood or oil or coal taken from throughout the geologic column. **Every** sample ever tested shows radioactivity, which means an age of only **thousands** (not millions) of years! Most test samples date within 20,000 years. The critics' attempted explanations of "contamination of samples" or "faulty testing techniques" simply cannot explain away this overwhelming evidence for a young earth. With corrections for the lower ratio of radioactive carbon in the past, the dates actually become even **younger**—to only a few thousand years. It's clear evidence that we have a young earth!

c. **Evidence from the earth's rotation**: The rotation of the earth is slowing down. The rotation rate can be measured by atomic clocks to the billionth of a second! If the earth were really 4-5 billion years old, its initial "spin" rate would have been so fast that the earth's shape would be greatly distorted. There would be huge bulges around the equator if a molten earth had been spinning that rapidly when solidifying. So the earth's rotation rate indicates that the earth could not have been "born" billions of years ago.

d. **Evidence from ocean and Dead Sea mineral content**: Oceans are salty because of the runoff of salt from the land. The salt content of the sea is constantly increasing. There should be much more sodium—and many other elements as well—in the oceans if the earth were billions of years old. The build-up of these elements **must** have started only a few thousand years ago.

The Dead Sea has no outlet, so the mineral content is easy to measure. It has been calculated that at the present rate of mineral deposit and evaporation, the Dead Sea could not possibly be more than 13,000 years old—and probably much less!

CONCLUSION

Why isn't this young earth evidence presented in our scientific journals and science textbooks? The reason is that the "Big Bang" and evolution are the prevailing secular scientific theories, and evidence that contradicts the prevailing scientific theories simply is pushed aside and not published. Scientists who do not conform to the prevailing theory actually jeopardize their careers. Promotions, university professorships, and research funds are not granted to scientists who differ from the big bang "party line." Many scientists (even Christians) simply capitulate, or give in, because the peer pressure and career pressure is so overwhelming. In the February, 1992, issue of *Scientific American,* Dr. Geoffrey Burbidge (a University of California physics professor) writes, "Big Bang cosmology is probably as widely believed as has been any theory of the universe in the history of Western civilization. It rests, however, on many untested and untestable assumptions . . . Yet the momentum that this bandwagon enjoys is overwhelming . . . Powerful mechanisms encourage conformity . . . It is extraordinarily difficult to get financial support or viewing time on a telescope unless one writes a proposal that follows the party line. Unorthodox papers are often denied publication for years . . . The same attitude applies to academic positions . . . This situation is particularly worrisome because there are good reasons to think the big bang model is seriously flawed."

Academic pride, peer pressure and ridicule may tempt Christians to conform to this world's current scientific theories, but the Bible warns us:

Romans 12:2: "And do not be conformed to this world, but be transformed by the renewing of your mind . . . "

1 John 2:15-17: "Do not love the world or the things in the world . . . For all that is in the world—the lust of the flesh, the lust of the eyes, and the pride of life—is not of the Father, but is of the world. And the world is passing away . . ."

If we come **without any presuppositions** to the evidence in God's Word (the Bible), and if we look **without any presuppositions** at the scientific evidence which is available in God's Work (nature), we will come to the conclusion that we have a young universe and a young earth, designed and brought into being just as the Bible describes.

CHAPTER ELEVEN

❖ ❖ ❖

DID GOD USE EVOLUTION OR PROGRESSIVE CREATION?

Can a Christian believe in God and evolution at the same time? Isn't it possible that God brought all the different kinds of plants and animals and even human beings into existence through the process of evolution? Some Christians honestly wonder about the method God used to bring about the great variety of life forms that we see in existence today.

The idea that God created a fully functional universe in six literal days is staggering to the natural way of thinking. Of course, non-Christian scientists completely reject such an idea. They believe that all living things came into being through the process of evolution: higher, more complex forms of life developed from the lower, less complex forms of life by themselves, without God, through natural selection of chance mutations over long periods of time. A true Christian could not believe in **atheistic** (no God) evolution. Some Christians, however, propose that God used evolution to bring about the variety of life forms in existence today ("theistic evolution"). And other Christians suggest that the days of Genesis 1 were actually long time periods or geologic ages in which God did creative acts ("progressive creation").

At different times during my education as a scientist, I (the author) held both of these latter two positions. However, I have come to believe that these positions distort the biblical account of creation, and require serious doctrinal compromise as well.

Of course an all-powerful God **could** have used any number of ways to bring life into existence, but **what does the Bible teach** about how God actually **did** bring life into being?

A. EVIDENCE AGAINST EVOLUTION FROM THE BIBLE

1. Biblical Chronology

A straightforward reading of the first 11 chapters of Genesis would indicate that God did **not** use evolution to create life.

a. Chronologies of Genesis 5 and Genesis 11: As we mentioned in Chapter 10, the family records (genealogies) of Genesis 5 and 11 don't allow for human life to be millions of years old. While there may be a few generational gaps in these lists, specific numbers of years are given, so there is little room for flexibility. There is absolutely **no** possibility that **millions** of years could be squeezed into these presumed gaps, and there is no biblical indication that human life began much more than about 6,000 years ago.

b. The sequence of creation in Genesis 1: The sequence of events in Genesis 1 does not fit either the theory of theistic evolution or the theory of progressive creation. According to the theory of evolution, for example, fish evolved before fruit-bearing trees, but according to Genesis 1:12 & 20 all plant life was created two days before all marine life. The theory of evolution postulates that birds evolved from reptiles. Millions of years were required for the scales, forelimbs and solid bones of reptiles to evolve into the feathers, wings and hollow bones of birds, and many more years of evolution were required before birds were able to fly. But the biblical record states that God brought birds into being on the 5th day— **before** reptiles, which came on the 6th day (Genesis 1:20, 25).

Progressive creationists postulate that the "days" of Genesis 1 represent geologic ages, or long periods of time. The problems are great for anyone who tries to fit a progressive creation theory into the Genesis record. One example: If the "days" of Genesis 1 were actually geologic ages, how long could the plants which appear in the "3rd geologic age" (the 3rd day) be able to survive while waiting for the coming of sunlight in the "4th geologic age" (the 4th day)?

2. Biblical Theology

a. The Biblical authors and the Lord Jesus: Jesus never viewed the early chapters of Genesis as symbolic. (See Matthew 19:4-6 and Luke 11:50-51 as examples.) Speaking of human beings, the Lord Jesus said, "From the beginning of creation God made them male and female" (Mark 10:6). By using the phrase, "But from the **beginning** of the creation," Jesus Himself ruled out millions of years of evolution or progressive acts of creation **before** the creation of humans.

Many biblical authors wrote about God's creative acts, and none of them ever considered the early chapters of Genesis as poetry, imagery or an allegory, or as representing long periods of time. Incidentally, Hebrew poetry has a definite structure to it, and the Creation account of Genesis 1 and 2 is not Hebrew poetry.

b. Interpretation of "Day" in Genesis 1: There is **no biblical indication** that the word *yom* (the Hebrew word for "day") in Genesis 1 is meant to be interpreted as anything other than a literal 24-hour day. Although in some contexts *yom* is used to convey something other than a 24-hour solar day ("The Day of the Lord," for example), the context of Genesis 1, with the use of the words "evening and morning," indicates 24-hour days. Even unbelieving Hebrew scholars are persuaded that the author of Genesis 1 intended to convey 24-hour days. The idea that because 2 Peter 3:8 says, "with the Lord one day is as a thousand years, and a thousand years as one day" we can substitute any amount of time for the word "day" anywhere in the Bible is "horrible hermeneutics"! Such interpretation is a serious misrepresentation of what Peter, the inspired writer, intended to teach!

In Exodus 20:11, Moses, the inspired writer, certainly intended to convey to his Hebrew audience that the universe was created in **six literal days**: "For in six days the LORD made the heavens and the earth, the sea and all that is in them, and rested the seventh day." If God had created in geologic ages, He would have not have inspired Moses to write the Hebrew words for "six days"—He could easily have had him write the Hebrew equivalent of "geologic ages"!

c. Creation of Eve: Some evolutionists have proposed that the creation of Adam out of "dust from the ground" is the Bible's use of figurative language to communicate evolution. If the story of the formation of Eve is also symbolic of woman being slowly formed through evolution, then God has certainly given us a very strange and misleading "symbolic" tale in Genesis 2:18-25!

   d. Doctrine of death: Death is the biggest and most serious theological problem facing the Christian who wishes to go along with the theories of theistic evolution or progressive creation. Even those people who believe in the so-called "gap theory" of Genesis 1 (see "iv" below) have serious theological problems when the matter of "death" is considered.

   i. The whole concept of evolution is based on the **deaths** of billions of weak or maladapted organisms, and the survival and advance of only the most fit specimens. However, Romans 5:12-14 teaches that death is the result of human sin and that human sin started with Adam—that is, death was not in the world before Adam and Eve sinned, as recorded in Genesis 3.

   ii. Those who hold to the theories of theistic evolution or progressive creation deny the biblical teaching that death came **after** the first human being was already in existence. They argue that Romans 5 refers only to human death, and not to non-moral deaths of millions of "lower" animals, primates and "humanoids" leading, over billions of years, up to man. But Romans 8:18-22 clearly indicates that the death and decay which we see in the natural world came about as a **result of human sin**.

   iii. The theories of theistic evolution and progressive creation portray God as an extremely cruel and inefficient Creator. If either of these theories is true, God is presented as "developing" life through a barbaric process of trial and error involving suffering, catastrophe, death, and a savage "tooth and claw" survival of the fittest. Is that a character description of the **God of the Bible**?

   iv. The "gap theory," (taught in the old Scofield Reference Bible and elsewhere), suggests that there was an original perfect creation in Genesis 1:1. This original creation became desolate and ruined because of divine judgment associated with Satan's fall, and during this chaotic "gap" (referred to in Genesis 1:2), all life died. The evidence of all this death is found in the fossil record of the geologic column, according to this view. Then God began a week of re-creation or reconstruction beginning with Genesis 1:3.

   Following are some problems with the gap theory:

a. Since animal fossils are found in the geologic column, the gap theory admits that there was **death** prior to mankind's sin in Genesis 3. Yet Genesis 3 states that death was introduced at the Fall of Man.

b. In addition, Romans 8:18-22 places a huge and serious question mark over the "Gap Theory" by indicating that **all** death is the result of the Fall of mankind recorded in Genesis 3.

c. Human artifacts are found in the geologic column, which forces gap theorists to come up with the idea of a so-called "pre-Adamic human race," for which there is no evidence. (The geologic column containing these artifacts is much better explained by the world-wide Flood of Noah's day, rather than either evolution or a proposed gap between Genesis 1:1 and 1:3.)

d. Ezekiel 28 indicates that Satan was in "Eden, the Garden of God" in his **unfallen** state. The Garden of Eden was not in existence in Genesis 1:1-2. It does not appear in Scripture until Day 6 of the Creation Week (Genesis 2:7-8). So the fall of Satan cannot be the cause of the so-called gap.

e. Genesis 1:31 tells us that "God saw everything that He had made, and indeed it was very good." If God knew that the earth already contained a geologic column with the record of past catastrophe and millions of years of violent death, could God have said that **everything** was "very good"?

B. EVIDENCE AGAINST EVOLUTION FROM NATURE

1. Evidence for recent plant and animal life

a. **Radioactive carbon dating**: This test dates former living materials, and can be cross-checked for calibration and accuracy by other dating methods, such as dendro-chronology (tree ring dating). What are the results? **Every** specimen ever tested from throughout the geologic column all over the world has shown radioactivity, thus indicating that the specimen is only thousands, not millions, of years old.

b. **Intact large molecules**: Some fossils contain organic matter that can be checked for the break-down of large molecules like proteins and DNA. If organic material is really millions of years old all the proteins and DNA should be completely broken down. However, both intact protein and DNA molecules have been found in both plant and animal fossils—

including dinosaur fossils! These facts indicate that these plants and animals lived only a few thousand years ago—not millions! Yet evolutionary theory states that dinosaurs have been extinct for over 100 million years! That's impossible!

c. Extinct fossil animals: Evolution assumes that certain extinct species (such as dinosaurs) must be very ancient. But sometimes "extinct" species show up unexpectedly, such as a 4,000 pound, 30 foot long "extinct" sea-dwelling plesiosaur carcass that was caught by Japanese fishermen in 1977!

d. Plant, animal and human fossils found in the same layer of the geologic column: In Utah, in the Cambrian layer (supposedly 550 million years before humans appeared on earth) a trilobite (an extinct marine invertebrate) fossil was found in the same layer as a fossilized human footprint. Recent "footprint" excavations in Texas and Russia have revealed that dinosaurs and humans lived during the same time period, not millions of years apart. This hotly contested evidence has still not been successfully refuted by secular scientists and new supporting evidence continues to mount.

e. Pre-Cambrian period fossils: The oldest fossil-bearing rocks are from the Cambrian period, where billions of fossils from the simplest organisms to highly complex organisms have all been found. But no multi-celled fossils are found in rocks older than the Cambrian layer. The supposed forerunners of the Cambrian fossils are **nowhere to be found**.

f. Transitional forms: Not only is there an explosion of fully formed multi-celled organisms in the so-called Cambrian period, but throughout the geologic column there are **no transitional forms**. There are no "halfway" fossils between invertebrates and vertebrates (life forms with skeletal structure). And there are no "half-way" fossils between "lower" vertebrates and "higher" vertebrates. For example, there are no fossil horses with 2½ toes or 1½ toes to show the supposed evolution of horses from multi-toed animals to horses with hooves. The well-touted archaeopteryx fossil is not a transitional form between reptiles and birds, but clearly an extinct bird. There are no transitional forms, or any other evidence of evolution.

2. Evidence for recent human life

a. Population statistics: Population statistics provide very powerful evidence for recent human life and for the reliability of the biblical records in the book of Genesis. In spite of wars, plagues and famines, worldwide human population has always increased. Using well-established equations and very conservative estimates, starting **one million years ago** with **one human male and female**, assuming each family had only 3 children and a 35 year generation length, and even factoring in wars and natural disasters, we find that the **known universe could not contain the number of people that would be alive now**!

Population statistics clearly show that there is just **no way** humans could have been in existence for 1,000,000 years! This extremely powerful evidence is not mentioned by evolutionary scientists, the popular press, textbooks, or "documentary" programs on educational television. Interestingly, calculations show that starting with eight people in 2500 B.C. (close to the date of the biblical Flood), and using figures in line with the Bible and the other historical records, the resulting population number is very close to the number of people on the earth today!

b. Fossil man: Paleontologists (scientists who study fossils) who believe in evolution claim to have found fossils of "ape-men," or "hominids," which are supposed to be the ancestors of true humans. The truth is, what they have found are fossils of true apes or fossils of true humans, but they have **never** found fossils of "ape-men" or "hominids." The "hominids" that are used by paleontologists to demonstrate evolution have been put together from portions of skeletons (sometimes only a few bones!) or from skeletal reconstruction of scattered bones which may not even belong to the same skeleton. In at least one case, a well-known paleontologist actually admits to reshaping a hip bone with an electric planer, so it would fit the skeleton and his theory that it **must** have come from a "hominid" which walked upright! The hip bone he re-shaped was, of course, actually the hip of a true ape. Imaginative and deceptive renditions of the supposed physical appearance of these "hominids" appear in textbooks and museum displays, causing most people to believe that full fossils of these hairy "ape/man" creatures were actually found and that they actually existed. Some examples of these deceptive practices are:

i. "Cro-Magnon man"— actually a true human, but has been misrepresented by artists to look like an ape-like man.

    ii. "Java man"— reconstructed of human and ape bones.

    iii. "Lucy"— created from a human knee bone and the upper body bones of a female ape. The knee bone was found over a mile apart from the other bones in different layers of sediment!

    iv. "Neanderthal man"— probably a true human. Artists took too many liberties with their supposed renditions of what this human looked like!

    v. "Nebraska man"— invented from one tooth, which was later found to be the tooth of a pig!

    vi. "Nutcracker man"— a true ape fossil found in East Africa. Since true human fossils and human artifacts were found in rock layers **below** the ape fossil, it could not possibly be a hominid, based on evolutionary theory.

    vii. "Piltdown man"— a definite hoax, proved to be so after 41 years!

c. **"Cave Men"**: Cave dwellings and drawings on cave walls are **not** evidence of early "pre-human" creatures. Throughout human history, intelligent, civilized, fully human peoples have lived in caves. In fact, right up until modern times people have lived in caves (in Australia, Jordan and Turkey, for example), and many of these people still create beautiful artwork on cave walls!

d. The **"Eve Gene"**: In research on mitochondrial DNA (DNA received only from the mother), recent evidence has pointed to the existence of a common female ancestor for all humans, who lived only **thousands** (not millions) of years ago. Although they have called this evidence the "Eve Gene," unbelieving scientists do not actually believe this was the Eve of the Bible. In their view, all other potential mothers of homo sapiens died off. Molecular archaeology may indeed eventually prove that she **was** the Eve of the Bible!

e. **Human artifacts**: Artifacts are products of human (not "hominid") civilization, showing human intelligence. Dolls, screws, nails, iron bands, tools, cooking utensils, and hundreds of other artifacts of human life and industry have been found in many locations throughout the geologic column, in rock layers whose proposed dates are well before true humans are supposed to have existed.

C. EVIDENCE AGAINST EVOLUTION FROM SECULAR SCIENTISTS

The following quotes, stating problems with evolution, have been made by secular scientists who are "authorities" in the field of origins:

Quote: To suppose that the eye with all its inimitable contrivances for adjusting the focus to different distances, for admitting different amounts of light, and for the connection of spherical and chromatic aberration, could have been formed by natural selection, seems, I freely confess, absurd in the highest degree.

Quote: If it could be demonstrated that any complex organ existed which could not possibly have been formed by numerous, successive slight modifications, my theory would absolutely break down.

Scientist: Charles Darwin, *The Origin of Species,* J. M. Dent & Sons Ltd, London, 1971.

Quote: The extreme rarity of transitional forms in the fossil record persists as the trade secret of paleontology. The evolutionary trees that adorn our textbooks have data only at the tips and nodes of their branches; the rest is inference, however reasonable, not the evidence of fossils.

Scientist: Stephen J. Gould (Professor of Geology and Paleontology, Harvard University), "Evolution's Erratic Pace," *Natural History*, Vol LXXXVI(5), May 1977.

Quote: I regard the failure to find a clear "vector of progress" in life's history as the most puzzling fact of the fossil record . . . we have sought to impose a pattern that we hoped to find on a world that does not really display it.

Scientist: Stephen J. Gould, "The Ediacaran Experiment," *Natural History*, Vol 93, February 1984.

Quote: I think, however, that we must go further than this and admit that the only acceptable explanation is *creation*. I know that this is anathema to physicists, as indeed it is to me, but we must not reject what we do not like if the experimental evidence supports it.

Scientist: H. S. Lipson, (Professor of Physics, University of Manchester, UK), "A Physicist Looks at Evolution," *Physics Bulletin*, Vol 31, 1980.

Quote: The [evolutionary] origin of birds is largely a matter of deduction. There is no fossil evidence of the stages through which the remarkable change from reptile to bird was achieved.

Scientist: W. E. Swinton (British Museum of Natural History, London), "The Origin of Birds," Chapter 1, *Biology and Comparative Physiology of Birds*, A. J. Marshall (editor), Vol 1, Academic Press, New York, 1960.

Quote: It is not difficult to imagine how feathers, once evolved, assumed additional functions, but how they arose initially, presumably from reptilian scales, defies analysis.

Quote: Because of the nature of the fossil evidence, paleontologists have been forced to reconstruct the first two-thirds of mammalian history in great part on the basis of tooth morphology.

Scientist: Barbara J. Stahl (St. Anselm's College, USA), *Vertebrate History: Problems in Evolution*, McGraw-Hill, New York, 1974.

Quote: The family tree of the horse is beautiful and continuous only in textbooks.

Scientist: Heribert Nilsson, *Synthetische Artbildung*, Verlag CWE Gleerup, Lund, Sweden, 1954.

Quote: I still think that, to the unprejudiced, the fossil record of plants is in favor of special creation.

Scientist: E. J. H. Corner (Professor of Tropical Botany, Cambridge University, UK), "Evolution," *Contemporary Botanical Thought*, Anna M. MacLeod and L. S. Cobley (editors), Oliver and Boyd, for the Botanical Society of Edinburgh, 1961.

CONCLUSION

At first glance, theistic evolution may appear to be an ideal way to harmonize the theory of evolution with the early chapters of Genesis. However, a closer examination of the teaching of these chapters—and other Scriptures—indicates that such a harmonization is impossible. In the final analysis, it's either evolution **or** God's Word—you can't have it both ways!

Evolution has never been demonstrated in the laboratory and cannot be shown from the fossil record. Genetic variation should not be confused with evolution. God created the various "kinds" of Genesis 1 with the genetic capability of innumerable variations, but this is not evolution. For evolution to take place, new genetic information must be added. Mutations (the mechanism for evolution) have **never** added new genetic information.

True science is **not** in conflict with Scripture. The long ages needed for theistic evolution or any form of progressive creation are not in the Bible, nor are they proved by science. Biblical and scientific evidence **both** point to **recent life**.

❖ ❖ ❖

WAS THERE A
WORLD-WIDE FLOOD?

A. BIBLICAL EVIDENCE FOR THE FLOOD

1. Fact of the Flood

In Genesis 6-9, the Bible teaches that there was a great, world-wide, catastrophic Flood. In Genesis 6 God announced that there would be a great flood in which all of mankind and animals on the entire earth would be wiped out. He gave the reason for this terrible judgment—-the sinful hearts and wicked behavior of mankind.

2. Size of the Flood

a. Statements from the Bible

i. Genesis 6:5, 12, 13, 17 says, "Then the LORD saw that the wickedness of man was great in the earth, and that every intent of the thoughts of his heart was only evil continually . . . So God looked upon the earth, and indeed it was corrupt; for **all flesh** had corrupted their way on the earth . . . And God said to Noah, 'The end of **all flesh** has come . . . I will **destroy** them with **the earth** . . . I myself am bringing the flood of waters on the earth, to destroy from under heaven **all flesh** . . . **everything** that is on the earth shall die'" (emphasis added). Since the sin was worldwide, the judgment would also be worldwide.

ii. Genesis 7:1-3 states that the purpose of the ark (a huge, barge-like boat) was to keep Noah and his family, and the animals "alive on the face of the earth." If the Flood had been only a local flood, building a boat larger than several hundred railroad boxcars would certainly not have been necessary—surely some people and animals would have been able to escape over the hills to safety! Or God could have communicated to Noah to take his family and all the animals, and escape to a certain spot that would not be affected by the limited destruction of a "local" flood. (That's how God saved Lot and his family from the destruction of Sodom [see Genesis 19].)

iii. Genesis 7:18-23 says that "the waters . . . greatly increased on the earth, and the ark moved about on the surface of the waters . . . and all the high hills under the whole heaven were covered . . . All in whose nostrils was the breath of the spirit of life, all that was on the dry land, died . . . Only Noah and those who were with him in the ark remained alive." Sounds like a world-wide Flood!

iv. Genesis 9:12-14 indicates that God gave the rainbow as a sign that there would never be another world-wide Flood. If the biblical Flood was only a local catastrophe then God lied because there have been many devastating localized floods since Noah's time. Psalm 104:6-9 also indicates that after the Flood God, ". . . set a boundary . . ." which the waters could not cross. The Flood must have been global.

b. Arguments from the Bible

i. Moses, the inspired author of Genesis, and the apostle Peter, in 2 Peter 3, certainly meant to convey to their readers that there was a world-wide Flood. Did they try to deceive their readers—or were they themselves mistaken, and not actually inspired by the Holy Spirit after all?

ii. Jesus believed in a Flood of global proportions. In Matthew 24:5-39, Jesus compared conditions surrounding His second coming to the world-wide Flood and its catastrophic proportions.

iii. Under divine inspiration, Peter wrote of a Flood that deluged and destroyed the entire world. "By the word of God the heavens were of old, and the earth standing out of water and in the water, by which the world that then existed perished, being flooded with water" (2 Peter 3:5-6). Peter then compared the past total destruction of the earth—by water—to the future total destruction of the earth—by fire.

3. Mechanics of the Flood

a. Water for the Flood:

Is there enough rain to destroy the earth today? If all the water that is presently in the atmosphere came down at once, it would form a sheath of water less than a foot in depth around the earth. The Bible indicates that there were two sources for the origin of the huge amount of water: "the fountains of the great deep were broken up, and the windows of heaven were opened. And the rain was on the earth forty days and forty nights" (Genesis 7:11-12).

i. **"The fountains of the great deep"**: Subterranean water was released, maybe even shooting up into the air like geysers. This statement also indicates worldwide earthquakes, and worldwide volcanic activity.

ii. **"The windows of heaven"**: This phrase may refer to a "canopy" of water vapor which surrounded the earth before the Flood. This type of "canopy" would have caused the sun's heat to be more equally distributed around the earth so that a semitropical climate would have existed around the earth—like a giant greenhouse. The "windows of heaven" being opened may refer to the collapse of such a canopy, and the water precipitated as rain for forty days and nights. Certain Scriptures indicate the distinct likelihood of a water vapor canopy, for example:

Genesis 1:6-8 speaks of a "firmament" [space] that separated "the waters above" [the canopy] from "the waters below" [the seas]. Today the water is in the atmosphere, not above it. "The waters above" may very well be speaking of a "canopy" of water that was present around the earth.

Genesis 2:6 says that there was no rain before the Flood, just a mist from the ground to water the earth. A canopy around the earth would have created a very different climate, somewhat like a greenhouse without rain.

Genesis 9:11-13 tells about the rainbow, God's sign that there would never again be a universal Flood. Before the Flood a rainbow would have been impossible, because there was no rain. If a canopy was precipitated during the Flood, the major source of water for a global flood would be gone. A worldwide flood can never occur again because the earth's present atmosphere contains only a limited amount of water, which precipitates periodically as rain. So the rainbow was a very appropriate sign!

Genesis 8:22 speaks of new climatic conditions. If a canopy no longer shielded the earth, the world-wide year-round semi-tropical greenhouse effect would be gone. Instead there would be seasons: "seedtime and harvest, cold and heat, summer and winter."

Genesis 11 records show that there was a striking drop in the length of people's lives after the Flood. If a canopy was present before the Flood, the earth would have been shielded from the sun's dangerous cosmic radiation—especially the rays which are most active in the aging process. The disappearance of a canopy shield may explain the shorter life-spans after the Flood.

2 Peter 3:6-7 speaks of a world cosmography (the constitution and order of the heavens and earth) before the Flood, which was different from "the present heavens and earth."

b. Natural phenomena following the Flood

i. Amount of water: Where did all the water go after the Flood? It's still here! There is significant evidence that there is much more water on the earth's surface now than in the past.

Ice at the Poles: Some of the water is frozen in the ice caps at the North and South Poles. These ice caps definitely did not exist in the past. There is clear and convincing geologic evidence that both the North and South Poles were once semi-tropical in climate.

Oceans: Erosion (the kind of erosion that does not take place under water) of the continental shelves and sea mounts shows that the ocean water is much deeper now than it was in the past.

Formation of mountains: After the Flood, the greater weight of water draining into the oceans caused the ocean floors to sink and the mountains to rise as the earth was coming into isostatic equilibrium. Very high mountains did not exist before the Flood, but came into being by the volcanic and tectonic activity during and after the Flood. (Tectonic activity refers to the forces which cause the Earth's crust to buckle and fold, and gradually build mountain ranges.) Psalm 104:6-8 suggests the aftermath of the Flood: "the waters were standing above the mountains. At Your rebuke they fled . . . the mountains rose; the valleys sank down . . ." (NASB).

ii. Continental drift: The continents rest on tectonic plates which are "drifting." During and following the Flood, the movement of these plates would have been much greater than today. This could have been because of greater tectonic subduction (one tectonic plate sliding under another) in association with the break-up of the "fountains of the deep," as well as the forces bringing the earth to isostatic conditions (equalizing pressures) with the great increase of water on the surface. Although movement is greatly reduced now, it still exists. For example, the plate on which India sits is still moving into the plate on which Eurasia sits, causing tectonic activity in the Himalayan mountains. Immediately following the Flood the "collision" of those tectonic plates would have caused great uplift, resulting in the mountains of the Himalayan range, including Mount Everest.

iii. **Migration of species**: Why are kangaroos found only in Australia? Most likely there were land bridges between the continents following the Flood, particularly during the "Ice Age" which developed soon after the Flood, when a great amount of water was precipitated at the Poles as snow and tied up as ice. Land bridges allowed the faster moving species to spread out before continental drift, tectonic activity and melting of the glaciers cut off certain land bridges. (The glaciers began to recede as a result of the buildup of the carbon dioxide layer in the atmosphere which has resulted in a significant greenhouse effect since the time of the flood.) Marsupials (such as kangaroos) are the fastest moving species because they carry their young in pouches. There are fossil marsupials (including kangaroos) found in many parts of the world, showing that marsupials existed around the world before the Flood.

iv. **Climate changes**: Fossils at both Poles, seams of coal at the South Pole, and oil deposits found above the Arctic Circle are clear evidence that warmer conditions existed there in the past. The presence of a surrounding water vapor canopy would have created a greenhouse effect—a temperate climate over all the earth before the Flood. Genesis 8:22 (**after the** Flood) gives us the first mention of climate—"cold and heat." There is **no other** good explanation of why the climate at the Poles was formerly temperate!

v. **Frozen mammoths**: In Siberia and Alaska complete frozen animals have been found entombed in ice, flesh and all, with undigested food still preserved in their stomachs. These animals were frozen so quickly that, occasionally, their flesh has been thawed and used as meat to feed sled dogs! In order to get the radical conditions necessary to freeze such huge animals so rapidly, the change in climate must have been **very** rapid and extreme—a cataclysmic event. Science has found **no** adequate explanation. However, the theory that the water vapor canopy precipitated first at the Poles, coming in as super-cooled ice fog, quickly freezing the animals, and bringing about a permanent climate change is a distinct possibility.

Another possibility is that a phase of the post-Flood "ice age" in the far northern hemisphere could have begun quite suddenly because of post-flood tectonic activity. The sudden cutoff of warm ocean waters from tropical currents would result in a rapid drop in temperature.

vi. Ice Age: The book of Job (probably the earliest written book of the Bible) mentions that Job knew of great amounts of ice (Job 37:10; 38:29-30). Because of the rapid build-up of the polar ice cap following the Flood there would have been an "ice age" in the first few hundred post-Flood years. The glaciers would have covered a good portion of present-day Europe and North America. This would have lasted until the carbon dioxide layer around the earth built up sufficiently to give a measure of "greenhouse effect."

vii. Age of trees: Trees are the oldest living things, and redwoods, sequoias and bristle-cone pines are the oldest trees. The oldest living thing on earth today, a bristle-cone pine in northern California, is dated by scientists at 4500-4600 years old. That tree and others in that forest are **first generation trees**—there are no stumps or remains of trees that go back any further. These trees started to grow 4500-4600 years ago—-the time when biblical chronology indicates the Flood occurred! These trees apparently grew from seeds that survived the Flood and implanted themselves in the new sediments.

B. ARCHAEOLOGICAL EVIDENCE FOR THE FLOOD

The search for Noah's ark continues in the Ararat mountains of eastern Turkey. Reports of sightings have continued over many years, but no indisputable evidence has been produced thus far. Bad weather and risky political situations create problems in getting expeditions to that part of Turkey. It is possible that the remains of Noah's ark still exist and are being preserved in the ice of Mt. Ararat. In due time, God may melt back the glaciers to reveal the evidence. However, whether or not Noah's ark is found, skeptics will still refuse to believe in the Genesis Flood.

C. ANTHROPOLOGICAL EVIDENCE FOR THE FLOOD

Virtually all societies and cultures in the world today have a traditional story in their folklore of a worldwide flood that took place in ancient times. These traditions include the detail that most people died, and only a few escaped. The fact that there is a common "Great Flood" tradition in the folklore of peoples all around the world strongly indicates that there **must** have been an event in the past which **started** these traditions—namely, the historical worldwide Flood recorded in the Bible. Noah and his descendants would have told and re-told the story of the Flood to the next generation, and although details in these Flood traditions became distorted over the years, the world-wide tradition itself is good evidence of the historical event. The Babylonian account of the Great Flood (known as the Gilgamesh Epic) was written before the time of Moses, but the biblical account, written by Moses under the inspiration of the Holy Spirit, is the true account of the actual event.

D. GEOLOGICAL EVIDENCE FOR THE FLOOD

Scientists who believe in evolution accept the theory that the geologic column (represented by the rock layers of the earth, called geologic strata) and the fossils contained in these rock layers present a record of evolutionary development over very long periods of time. (See the Table in Chapter 10). Other scientists who have a high view of Scripture believe that the earth's rock layers were laid down primarily during the Flood, since at least 75% of the earth's exposed surface is sedimentary rock, which is formed from sediments settling out of **water**. In other words, these rock layers were laid down during a relatively short period of time, and the fossils in these strata are evidence of death during the Flood, **not** evidence of evolution.

1. Stratified Rock

a. Construction of stratified rock:

Sedimentary rock, formed from sediments that settled out of moving water and then hardened, covers at least 75% of the earth's exposed surface, and at least 95% of the earth's fossils have been found in sedimentary rock. Just the fact that so much of the earth is covered by rock composed of sediments that settled out from **water** is strong evidence for a global Flood.

b. Characteristics of stratified rock:

i. Deformation of sediments: In numerous places throughout the earth, many rock layers are smoothly bent or folded together, without cracking or breaking, like several blankets or layers of Play-doh (a colorful modeling clay) placed on top of one another and then folded over. We all know that soft blankets or layers of Play-doh fold over without cracking or breaking. However, **rock** layers would **not** smoothly bend or fold together unless **all** the layers were soft and pliable **at the same time**, as would have been the case soon after the Flood. If the strata had built up and hardened over many millions of years, with long periods of time between each layer, the hardened rock layers would have cracked and broken when tectonic forces bent them. It is **impossible** to get smooth folds in already hardened rock layers.

ii. Boulders: Boulders are pieces of rock that have been rounded and worn smooth by being tumbled along in moving water, such as a river or flood waters. The inclusion of boulders throughout the geologic column indicates powerful water action throughout the time when the column was building up. This fact fits in well as evidence for a universal Flood, since many boulders would be produced and deposited in sediments by the very strong water action of the rising Flood. It's hard to explain all the boulders if the geologic column represents millions of years of slow and gradual build-up.

iii. Inclusion of fossils: Does every tree or animal that dies become a fossil? No! Rapid burial under sediments is required, or else the dead object would just rot away and not be fossilized. The fact that fossils are included in the geologic strata is clear evidence of **rapid** buildup of sediments from catastrophic water action.

iv. Conformities: "Conformities" are sharp, clean dividing lines in the strata between layers of rock, with no evidence of erosion (wearing away by exposure to the atmosphere) between the layers. Conformities are evidence of a **rapid** build-up of layers of sediments. There are mostly conformities throughout the strata all over the world—evidence for a worldwide Flood. In fact, anywhere in the world we can trace our way from the bottom to the top of the rock layers through conformities, showing that the geologic column was laid down and built up **continuously**. There are no **un**conformities (evidence of erosion between layers) that extend all around the earth. They are limited in extent. If the geologic column were really the record of evolution, we would expect to find mostly unconformities, with much evidence of weathering and erosion between layers, because (in the evolutionary view) long periods of time are required for the different layers of sediment to build up and evolution to take place. In the

"Flood geology" scenario, we should expect to find mostly conformities, as we do, but there would also be some unconformities in the geologic column, because portions of the earth's newly deposited sediments would be periodically exposed due to the tidal effects of the increasing Flood.

c. Carving of stratified rock

Meandering (winding or twisting) rivers which cut sharply through rock layers are called "incised meanders," and show evidence of **rapid** carving when the sediments were soft, not slow carving of solid rock over thousands of years. This is because meandering rivers simply **cannot** cut down through the **solid** rock with a twisting, meandering pattern. Also, many canyons (such as the Grand Canyon) could have been formed relatively rapidly by a large volume of water carving soft sediments, as would be the case in the continental drainage and run-off of the Flood waters. Consider the following modern day example. In **less than a week** a canyon covering 25 square miles was carved by mud flows in the soft ash and sediment layers deposited by the volcanic eruption of Mount St Helens in 1980! The carving of stratified rock around the world is good evidence for a global flood.

2. Widespread Formations

In the geologic column there are huge formations, containing similar fossils and the same materials, showing that each formation must have been deposited from the **same** source at the **same** time during a **major** catastrophe. Two examples: The "Dakota Formation" covers 200,000 square miles in the western US; the "Morrison Formation" reaches from Canada to Texas, covering at least 400,000 square miles. No local flood could produce such **huge** formations.

3. Numerous Turbidites

Around the world there is geologic evidence of many "turbidite" layers. Turbidites are formed by underwater mudflows or underwater landslides or "avalanches" of masses of silt and mud that flow rapidly and build up quickly into a layer—in **hours**, not long eras of time! The existence of turbidites in the sedimentary rock layers around the world is evidence of a global catastrophic Flood.

E. PALEONTOLOGICAL EVIDENCE FOR THE FLOOD

Paleontology is the study of fossils. **Everything** about fossils fits in well with a global Flood!

1. The Formation of Fossils

Fossils are formed only when dead objects are buried quickly under pressure in sediments, such as in a mudslide or mud flow (very consistent with flood conditions).

2. The Number of Fossils

The geologic column is **loaded** with fossils—millions and millions of fossils. If there must be rapid burial and quick buildup of sediments to obtain fossils, and the geologic strata are loaded with fossils, doesn't it make sense to consider that the geologic strata layers resulted from a catastrophic global Flood? Does it make sense to automatically assume that they are the result of millions of years of slow evolution?

3. The Size of Fossils

Large animal fossils (such as huge entire dinosaurs, elephants, etc.) are found in the rock layers, indicating a very large flood and rapid burial. These large fossils are good evidence of the worldwide biblical Flood.

4. The Types of Fossils

a. "Polystrate" fossils: Polystrate fossils extend through more than one geologic layer. For example, a fossilized tree trunk may stand fairly upright and extend through several rock layers. This shows that the layers **had** to be laid down in fairly quick succession, or the tree would have rotted before the next layer was laid down. A dead tree couldn't remain exposed for millions—or even thousands—of years while the sediments slowly built up around it! The existence of polystrate fossils is strong evidence of the rapid buildup of rock layers.

b. Fossilized "ephemeral markings": Prints of raindrops, water ripples, bird tracks, etc., are present all through the rock layers. These markings are easily washed or weathered away and must be captured and buried **quickly** to be preserved. They are **clear** evidence of **very** rapid buildup of layers. Incidentally no hail marks have been found in the geologic column. If the geologic column really represented millions of years, fossilized hail-prints would certainly be observed throughout the column.

5. The Age of Fossils

The organic matter remaining in some fossils can be dated with radioactive carbon, and fossils thus examined show they are only thousands —not millions—of years old. This puts all plant and animal fossils within the biblical time-frame for the global Flood.

6. The Suddenness of Fossils

There is a sudden appearance of all types of fossils in the geologic column. There is no evidence of evolution, such as single-celled organisms gradually moving to more and more complex forms of life as we move up through the sedimentary rock layers. The so-called "Cambrian explosion" of multiple life forms still has no logical naturalistic explanation. The sudden appearance of fossils overwhelmingly supports the biblical record of a worldwide flood. It does not support the theory of evolution.

7. The Perfection of Fossils:

No transitional forms ("missing links") have been found! For example, the archaeopteryx is not a transitional form between reptiles and birds—it's an extinct bird with wings and feathers. No fossils of reptiles with scales evolving into feathers or limbs partially evolved into wings have ever been uncovered. In fact, as more fossils are found, the boundaries between species have become even more defined!

8. The Sequence of Fossils:

The geologic column as proposed by evolutionary theory is found nowhere on the face of the earth. In fact in many places around the world we can find **any** layer of the geologic column "out of order" at the top! In looking for evidence of a worldwide Flood, we should **expect** to find exactly what we do find in the rock layers. Consider the following:

a. **"Inverted order"**: Fossils of "lower" forms of life are found higher in the geologic column than "higher" forms of life, and the same species may be found in many different layers. This is exactly what you would expect to find as a result of a sudden catastrophic Flood, where many various forms of life are overtaken by the flood waters and buried helter-skelter throughout the various sediment layers. Fossils of "higher" forms of life—**with organic matter still remaining**—have been found in rock which is supposedly millions of years old!

b. **Fossil graveyards**: Fossil graveyards, with many species buried together, have been found all over the earth, indicating that many species were overtaken by a huge catastrophic flood.

c. **Specific gravity**: The fact that there are more fossils of "lower," less complex species (invertebrates such as clams and shellfish) in lower rock layers of the geologic column does not indicate evolution. In a worldwide Flood, the "lower," less complex forms of life would be trapped and buried in the lower sediments because they are denser and settle out of moving water before the "higher" forms, which are lower in specific gravity.

d. **Ecologic zones**: While we should expect to find marine fossils on the tops of mountains (which we do) as a result of a worldwide flood, in general the "lower" marine life fossils should be found, as they are, in the lower sedimentary rock layers. This stands to reason, because life in the ecological zone around sea level is bound to have been buried in the early stages of a global flood.

e. **Mobility**: A greater percentage of "higher," more complex animal species in the higher rock layers is not necessarily evidence of evolution. Rather it is evidence that these species had the intelligence and mobility to run to higher ground and escape a catastrophic flood longer than the less mobile, less complex species. This is exactly what we would expect the evidence to show.

f. **Entrapment**: The "higher," more complex species would have been more likely to drown and float on top of the water, rather than become entrapped and fossilized along with the "lower," less complex species. Not only would the "higher" forms of life escape from the Flood longer, but because of more hydrodynamic drag (caused by limbs extending from the body), higher forms of life would be more likely to float and decompose, rather than becoming buried and fossilized. This would explain why there are relatively few human fossils compared to an overwhelming number of "lower life" fossils.

CONCLUSION

Faith, in biblical terms, is believing what God has revealed. "By faith Noah, being divinely warned of things not yet seen, moved with godly fear, prepared an ark for the saving of his household, by which he condemned the world and became heir of the righteousness which is according to faith" (Hebrews 11:7). When God told Noah to prepare an ark, Noah believed God. And he believed and obeyed God without a lot of evidence—in fact the Bible says he was warned about things that had never been seen before!

God asks us to believe what He has revealed—and for us it's not a blind leap of faith. **We have lots of evidence!** If we doubt God's Word and the evidence in nature for Creation and the Flood, it won't be long before we start to doubt a lot of other things about God's Word as well.

People may laugh at us for believing in a literal six-day Creation and the global Genesis Flood—but people laughed at Noah, too! Let's have the kind of courage that Noah displayed, and continue to believe what God has revealed in His Word and His works. **The evidence is there!**

READY TO GIVE AN ANSWER
RECOMMENDED READING LIST

A Ready Defense: The Best of Josh McDowell
Josh McDowell © 1990 Here's Life Publishers

The New Evidence that Demands a Verdict
Josh McDowell © 1999 Thomas Nelson

When Skeptics Ask
Norman L. Geisler & Ron Brooks © 1990 Victor Books

When Critics Ask
Norman L. Geisler & Therman How © 1992 Victor Books

Handbook of Christian Apologetics: Hundreds of Answers to Crucial Questions
Peter Kreeft & Ronald K. Tacelli © 1994 InterVaristy Press

Archaeology in Bible Lands
Howard F. Vos © 1977 Moody Press

Secrets of the Dead Sea Scrolls
Randall Price © 1996 Harvest House Publishers

The Case for Christ
Lee Strobel © 1998 Zondervan

The Battle for the Resurrection
Norman L. Geisler © 1989 Thomas Nelson

Icons of Evolution
Jonathan Wells © 1999 Regnery Publishing

The Genesis Record
John C. Whitcomb & Henry Morris © 1976 Puritan & Reformed

Scientific Creationism
Henry Morris © 1974 Creation Life Publishers

Darwin on Trial
Philip E. Johnson © 1991 InterVarsity Press

Darwin's Black Box: The Biochemical Challenge to Evolution
Michael J. Behe © 1996 The Free Press

Earth's Most Challenging Mysteries
Reginald Daly © 1972 The Craig Press

Bones of Contention
Marvin L. Lukenow © 1992 Baker Book House

Evolution: The fossils still say no
Duanne T. Gish Ph. D. © 1995 Institute for Creation Research

The Revised and Expanded Answers Book
Don Balten Ph. D. (editor) © 2000 Master Books

In the Minds of Men: Darwin and the New World Order
Ian T. Taylor © 1987 TFE Publishing

Origin By Design
Harold G. Coffin with Robert H. Brown © 1983 Review and
Herald Publishing Association

Evolution: A Theory in Crisis
New developments in science are challenging orthodox Darwinism
Michael Denton © 1985 Adler & Adler

Starlight and Time
D. Russell Humphreys © 1994 Master Books

It's a Young World After All: Exciting Evidences for Recent Creation
Paul D. Ackerman © 1986 Baker Book House

Creation and Time
A Report on the progressive creationist book by Hugh Ross
Mark Van Bebber & Paul S. Taylor © 1994 Eden Productions

Unlocking the Mysteries of Creation
Dennis R. Petersen © 2002 Master Books